Acclaim for **WHAT'S GOING ON? HOW CAN WE HELP?**

I0026221

# WHAT'S GOING ON?

# HOW CAN WE HELP?

THE CONSEQUENCES OF CAPITALISM
AND ACTIONABLE STEPS TOWARDS A
HEALTHY AND SUSTAINABLE FUTURE

FREEQUILL

# ILLUMINATE
# .PRESS.

BRIGHT IDEAS TOWARDS A HEALTHY
AND SUSTAINABLE FUTURE

1st Edition, 2018

ISBN:
Paperback     978-1-7752528-0-1
Electronic    978-1-7752528-1-8
Audio         978-1-7752528-2-5

This book is available as a paperback, eBook and audio book.
To find out more about our authors and books visit www.illuminatepress.com.

# Special Thanks

A huge, heartfelt thank-you to the people who search for injustice and seek to solve it, who hunt for power and fight to dissolve it, who create solutions to our challenges, and contribute to a better world. At times these may seem like incredibly ambitious goals but your strength, courage and commitment to being the change inspires us all.

"You may say that I'm a dreamer, but I'm not the only one."
-John Lennon

## Our Pledge

For every book sold we will help to plant ten trees to reduce soil degradation and air pollution as well as provide sustainable and healthy food for families in need. To facilitate this we have become an official partner with TREES.org. If there is any profit remaining we will continue to invest in sustainable and ethical projects that facilitate a brighter future.

# The Author

The principal author of this book goes by the alias FREEQUILL and chooses to remain anonymous.

"One person could change the whole world for the better, as long as they don't give a damn who gets the credit."
-Anonymous

# CONTENTS

# INTRODUCTION

The primary goal of this book is ambitious yet simple: to help people. In service of this we will explore some answers to questions that are becoming increasingly relevant:

## 1. WHAT'S GOING ON?

Our politicians often seem to focus on the symptoms rather than resolving the underlying causes–often applying new bandages to a potentially terminal infection. In part one we will delve deeper and uncover the true origins of our monetary system, consumer culture and capitalism. We will isolate the root causes, patterns and motivations behind our recurring obstacles. We will explore where we are at today and how we got here.

## 2. HOW CAN WE HELP?

If our current system is indeed failing, what's the alternative? In part two, we will look at a brand-new political framework: The Free System. This will be a chance to think big and explore creative solutions to our current challenges.

## 3. HOW CAN WE HELP TODAY?

To remain grounded and pragmatic, in part three we will discuss an array of smaller, practical solutions that you can implement straight away.

# The Journey

It often seems as though we are surrounded by a thickening mist of political, social and environmental crisis–increasing images that jar with our core values. What's more, it can feel as if our current systems prevent progress. Even a humble target such as sustainability can seem unreachable. Implementing collectively beneficial and scientifically proven baby-step solutions becomes an epic voyage.

Searching for change, we can feel heavy-laden as we scale the slopes of bureaucracy, pounded by the reign of ownership, shadowed by the black clouds of pessimism and pushed backwards by the bellowing force of our own antiquated systems.

Through the combination of isolating root causes and offering a brighter future with actionable, step-by-step plans of attack, this book offers you a chance to take the weight from your shoulders; and somewhere you can gather fresh resources, uncover alternative maps and explore brand-new horizons.

Like Janus, the two-faced Roman god of time, we can promote new beginnings by looking in opposing directions, both critically at our past and proactively towards our future. We will assess the systems we inherited from our forefathers while looking at alternatives that we would be proud to leave behind for our children.

The solutions don't have to come from fear, ego or a lack of resources. They can come from rational tools and techniques being developed and practiced by our leading scientists, pioneering thinkers, and compassionate activists.

In chapter one, we'll take an honest look at our current situation and introduce some useful tools to measure social progress. Let's dive in.

# PART I

# WHAT'S GOING ON?

# CHAPTER 1

# FRESH PERSPECTIVES

Are we 'progressing' too fast?

"In the midst of chaos, there is also opportunity."
-Sun Tzu

New viewpoints can enable us to circumvent seemingly insurmountable obstacles. They can allow us to see past the compromised lens of private monopolies. Fresh perspectives can unveil both answers and antidotes.

## Time Teaches

If we take a seemingly slow and gradual progression and compress it into a shorter timeframe, we can often more clearly notice a dramatic change in human behaviour. For example, someone may develop a serious illness but if the effects are gradual they may not be concerned by the increasing symptoms. They may start by not feeling 100% well, then less energetic, then go out less, then lose appetite, and so on. When a friend comes to visit, however, they will be shocked at the drastic changes in behaviour. They will be highly concerned as they have not been around to witness the gradual decline in wellbeing.

It is interesting to think of this effect with some things that have become part of our daily lives. A great example of this concept can be seen in Graham Burnett's book, *Permaculture: A Beginners Guide* [1]. In the following extract, Burnett remaps the history of Earth into just 30 days:

"If the 4.5 billion years of history on the earth could be compressed into 30 days, life in the form of a simple bacteria would appear on the tenth day and the first vertebrates would crawl the earth around the 25th day. Homo sapiens (the human species) would appear approximately one minute before midnight on the 30th day. The Industrial Revolution would occur during the last fraction of a second. In that instant, the face of the planet would have practically changed more than all of the previous periods."

This technique allows us to more objectively view where we came from and where we are heading. It allows us to distance ourselves and decide if we should explore a new path. It can inform us of the origins and evolution of many things that we may forget were once created. For example, by viewing the bigger picture we can see that there was once a time where we functioned without money, where consumer culture and advertising didn't exist, and when organic food was just called... food.

Let's explore this idea in more detail with a modern example. Let's compress the evolution of the smartphone, which until relatively recently was simply a concept, found only in science fiction. Its development, which spans decades, can be remapped into the following:

1973: The first mobile phone call was made. It was unveiled as a futuristic contraption, a large grey plastic block in the hands of Martin Cooper, a senior engineer at Motorola.

1986: The Motorola 4500x was released, a robust black box with a traditional phone receiver on top. No letters were included on the buttons as messaging technology had yet to be developed.

1989: The MicroTAC 9800x hit the market, a lighter handheld phone with an extendable aerial. The hefty price tag of over $3000 meant it was only used by the very wealthy.

1992: The Nokia 1011 was introduced at a more affordable price of around $500. It could send and receive text messages and boasted a large memory, storing up to 100 phone numbers.

While the range of mobile phone users increased, they were still mainly used by higher income adults, often for work-related purposes.

1998: More mobile phones were sold worldwide than cars and PCs combined.

1999: The Nokia 3210 was released. Aimed at a younger demographic, it was offered at a much lower price point and came preloaded with games, including the highly popular Snake.

2001: Now that a younger market had been reached, the industry began to grow exponentially. Accordingly, text messaging had increased by over 1000%, with 250 billion text messages sent worldwide.

2004: 500 billion text messages were sent.

2007: Texting was now one of the preferred forms of communication with nearly 2 trillion text messages sent worldwide. During this time phones were also increasingly feature rich. The Nokia N95, for example, had WiFi, an MP3 player, Bluetooth, GPS, a 5-megapixel camera and many other features.

2010: Twice as many children had mobile phones than they did in 2004.

2012: Apple sold an average of 340,000 iPhones per day.

It used to be uncommon to see someone using a mobile phone at home, or even in a public place, except to answer an important call. Within a very short timeframe it had now become 'normal' to see a train full of people staring into screens. During a one-to-one 'social' interaction, someone may frequently look at and use their phone.

2015 to present day: In a study by Nottingham Trent University, researchers asked participants aged 18 to 33 to estimate the amount of time they spend on their phones[2]. They then compared these self-reports to actual usage. The study revealed that the average participant checked their device 85 times a day, well beyond what they realized. A 2015 Gallup report found that nearly half of smartphone users couldn't imagine life without their phones[3]. And a report by the Huffington Post revealed that over 80% of people couldn't imagine a single day without them[4]. According to Professor of Psychology Steve Joordens, it is now the most widespread addiction in modern society[5].

The addictiveness of smartphones is facilitated by the ever-increasing array of purposefully highly addictive applications. Sean Parker, the ex-president of Facebook, recently went on record and confirmed that addiction is indeed the intention. He stated the thought process that went into building Facebook was all about: "How do we consume as much of your time and conscious attention as possible?"[6] He admitted that he and other smartphone application developers are consciously "exploiting a vulnerability in human psychology."[7] To which he adds, "God only knows what it's doing to our children's brains."[8]

In addition to addictions, smartphones are also frequently linked to insomnia, depression, isolation, anxiety[9] and even a decrease in cognitive performance. In a study by the University of Waterloo, researchers found "associations between heavy smartphone use and lowered intelligence."[10] Researchers from the University of Copenhagen noted how increased use of technology in everyday life can be "damaging the brain ... and lowering your IQ."[11] And recently, the University of Chicago revealed that the mere presence of a smartphone can significantly impede cognitive capacity. They concluded the following: "Results from two experiments indicate that even when people are successful at maintaining sustained attention–as when avoiding the temptation to check their phones–the mere presence of these devices reduces available cognitive capacity."[12]

Mobile devices also create a discrete conduit for personal attacks. Recent reports from i-SAFE state that over 25% of adolescents and teenagers have been repeatedly bullied through their smartphones or the Internet, and well over half of them do not inform their parents[13].

Bullying and a general sense of isolation didn't originate from smartphones, but they can greatly facilitate it. In a 2017 Atlantic article, Jean Twenge explains: "Today's teens may go to fewer parties and spend less time together in person, but when they do congregate, they document their hangouts relentlessly–on Snapchat, Instagram, Facebook. Those not invited to come along are keenly aware of it."[14] It seems as though our children can now grow up on a 24-hour reality TV show. And through the amount of views, shares, comments and likes, they can receive a running update of their popularity score.

The rise of a cyber generation might explain the rapidly climbing rates of teen depression and suicide[15]. Perhaps this is why Steve Jobs, CEO and co-founder of Apple, reportedly didn't allow his children to use an iPad[16].

New technological points of entry also create opportunities for cybercriminals. During a BBC interview in 2015[17], former CIA intelligence contractor Edward Snowden revealed how smartphones can be remotely taken over. In the 2016 show *State of Surveillance*[18], HBO asked a known hacker to remotely access a phone belonging to one of their reporters to prove that the technology exists. The hacker was able to commandeer the reporter's phone without him noticing. He was able to record his live calls, monitor his web browsing and call history, track his location, and activate the phone's microphone and cameras at will. They also noted how the software used to perform the hack was becoming more accessible.

Most smartphone owners keep their devices with them 24-hours a day, 7 days a week. When they sleep it is next to their head as an alarm clock; when they are jogging it provides them with a soundtrack; when they are driving it narrates the directions, and many are glued to them at home as they access 'social' media, TV, games and internet browsers. There are even products in development that will enable us to use smartphones in the shower[19].

Smartphones are becoming universal tools we use to acquire news, to study, to entertain ourselves, to pass the time, to structure our days and to create and define our relationships.

In only a handful of years, these new devices have found their way into our pockets, and we rarely question how they got there. Imagine that you slipped into a coma not long after the first mobile phone came on the market. Were you to wake up today, what would be your reaction to seeing every single face, regardless of age, gender, race or background, all silently staring into a glowing object in the palm of their hand?

I am not out to vilify smartphones. This was simply an example of remapping time. This is not a call for slamming on the brakes nor pressing the not-so-fast button. I am certainly not suggesting we cease technological developments. This would be a huge discredit to, among other things, the fantastic advances within the medical and sustainable energy sectors. I am proposing that we regularly assess our progress and the corresponding consequences to the environment, our health and social behaviour.

## Visitor's Viewpoint

"There is no energy crisis, food crisis or environmental crisis. There is only a crisis of ignorance."
-Richard Buckminster Fuller

Another useful technique to gain a fresh perspective is to imagine yourself as a tourist or visitor to Earth. Imagine you knew nothing of our history, media or political and economic systems. Let's suppose that you start by surveying your surroundings. You look at the land, the oceans, the natural resources, and the population. In an attempt to decipher political systems, you gather some basic facts to assess practical limitations. You come to the following conclusions:

· There are enough natural sustainable resources on this planet for everyone to live in comfort.
· There is sufficient land and agricultural knowledge for everyone to enjoy healthy, sustainable meals.
· And there are enough hours in the day for people to spend quality time with friends and family.

From your initial, surface-level assessment, you might determine that there aren't any practical limitations to a sustainable and fair society. Therefore, what would a visitor think when they begin to delve deeper and examine our economic and political systems? To explore this, let's look at some facts regarding sustainability and equality:

Sustainability
· The world population increases by more than 246,000 every day.[20]
· The current daily demand for oil is 93 million barrels.[21]
· Every day we lose 80,000 acres of rainforest.[22]
· Enough plastic is thrown away each year to circle the earth four times.[23]
· And we are currently depleting natural resources 60% faster than the planet can renew.[24]

Earth is a finite space and yet many of our current systems treat it as though we can continuously take and expand without limits. Some form of symbiotic relationship* with our natural resources is not a 'naïve utopia' nor a 'hippie dream'; it is a critical component of survival.

Equality
· CEOs earn 774 times as much as minimum wage earners.[25]

---

* A symbiotic relationship is one which benefits both parties.

10

· 6 private corporations control 90% of the media in the U.S.[26]
· Large businesses spend over $2.5 billion on lobbying* each year.[27]
· 46 million people are currently living as slaves*.[28]
· And the poorest half of the earth's population owns just 1% of the earth's wealth.[29]

Credit Suisse's economic research on wealth distribution in 2016 shows that eight individuals–with a combined capital of $426 billion–have as much wealth as 3.6 billion people[30]. In other words, 8 people have as much money as around half of all the people on this planet combined. That's the number of people it takes to fill a single SUV. That's not even enough people to start a soccer, football or baseball team. There are more people in the Wu-Tang Clan* than the number of people who collectively own 426 billion dollars.

Our vision can become compromised as it can be difficult to see the wood for the trees. By reviewing the basic inputs and outputs of our systems we can deduce that there is a vast amount of room for improvement. It's incredibly beneficial to think what it would look like from an outsider's perspective. One who is not affiliated with a geographical, religious or political alliance, or any number of potentially divisive narratives.

After gaining this fresh perspective of solely looking at the numbers, it is useful to pose further questions such as: If you had the choice would you choose our current system? Are you offered an option for a real alternative? Is this the best we can do?

Some illnesses are currently incurable as we lack the knowledge. And there are other issues in life where we lack the resources. Poverty and unsustainable acts, on the other hand, are 100% curable.

If we continue to think of ourselves as tourists on this planet, how would we classify our current systems?

"This is the world we know today–the world of capitalism and consumerism.

---

* Lobbying means to influence the decisions of public officials, notably politicians and policymakers.

* Someone is in slavery if they are forced to work through mental or physical threat, owned by an 'employer', bought or sold as 'property', or physically constrained.

* The Wu-Tang Clan is a hip hop group from Staten Island, New York, with 9 members.

A world where one can enslave fellow humans, rape the planet and be praised for their good business sense."

-Lidiya Kirilova

If we define a dystopia as a "place or state in which everything is unpleasant or bad, typically a totalitarian or environmentally degraded one"*, then this can accurately describe much of our world today. The chances are that in the city closest to you there are many people without homes who sleep on the cold, hard streets and who search through our discarded waste for survival. In many cases, these people have mental health problems, physical disabilities and traumatic backgrounds[31], and yet they are not provided with care. Our systems become totalitarian* when our leaders ignore the people and favour the wealthy voices of large corporations. And there is mounting evidence that our current state is an environmentally degraded one as we rapidly reduce biodiversity. We are polluting our air, soil and water. We are depleting finite natural resources–the vital ingredients of life.

There are currently several private corporations developing commercial space flight services, such as Blue Origin, Virgin Galactic, and Space X–a company that plans to build settlements on Mars within 10 years. Within our lifetimes it is looking increasingly likely that we will become a multi-planetary species. However, on Earth, our home planet, one which is perfect for life and abundant with renewable resources, our political systems fail miserably to feed and provide for the people. We spend billions looking for life on other planets and trillions destroying the ingredients for life on our home planet.

Massively upgrading our current political systems is vital and possible. Potential solutions shouldn't be automatically branded as an unattainable utopia; it should be viewed for what it is: a movement where we aim for a better scenario. Labelling the quest for improvement as naïve often promotes the illusion that our current issues are incurable. The truth is, we can all become part of a solution. And our collective health and futures are a far more

---

* Oxford Dictionary definition.

* A totalitarian system is one which is centralised and dictatorial.

12

noble goal than corporate profit.

"Since periods of change such as the present one come so rarely in human history, it is up to each of us to make the best use of our time to help create a happier world."
-The Dalai Lama

By learning from our mistakes we can make things right going forward. Rather than frantically filling the cracks that appear all over an ancient system, we can solve the root causes of our issues. We can start by gaining a fresh perspective and acknowledging where we are at today. Then we can explore the various ways to implement positive change. We don't have to carry the weight of the world on our shoulders nor ignore our human urge to help. Each of us can implement various methods to be part of a larger solution. We will discuss these in detail in the chapters to come–but first, we need more data.

What are the recurring patterns and themes behind our current challenges?

# CHAPTER 2

# THE ROOT OF IT ALL

Where did money come from?

"Money is one of the most successful stories ever told, because it's the story that almost everybody believes in."
-Yuval Noah Harari

Throughout our history we have been convinced that we need to buy things that belong to no one. The raw components for survival became commodities. Private corporations claimed the right to capture and own naturally produced resources. They then created contracts in order for you to obtain 'their' items. Now everything has a price tag. Forests, rivers and even mountains belong to private corporations and wealthy individuals.

## Having and Owning

"Our planet has plenty of resources to provide for everyone, the only thing we're short of, it seems, is money."
-Colin R. Turner

We wouldn't say that we 'own' sunsets as these are things we can all experience, benefit from and share. However, there was also a time when we wouldn't say that people could 'own' land. What does it mean to have or own something?

Ownership within capitalism can create an advantage over others. It suggests the capture or purchase of something that was once freely available. It facilitates a concentration of power, evident throughout our history: Egyptian Pharaohs, monarchies and, now, multinational corporations. Ownerships frequently encroach on our individual and collective freedoms.

It can be hard to imagine a world where we can redefine the concepts of having and owning as we have become so separated from our natural resources that we have started to view them as inherently owned. And it is hard for many to imagine a world without money as it has become deeply ingrained into our daily lives. It makes up our fears, worries, goals and ideologies. Money has shaped our way of life and our very understanding of purpose and success.

It is important for us to remember that in the approximate 250,000-year timeline of Homo sapiens, the concept of money has only been with us for around 6,000 years. When put into perspective, one can see that money, capitalism, the Industrial Revolution, and the transition from family and community to state and the market are just a tiny fraction of our collective history.

While we may view the period before money as a primitive 'caveman-esque' era, this would be incredibly inaccurate. Early humans enjoyed permanent settlements, advanced agriculture, science, art, sports and a vast array of hobbies, traditions and cultures. And even today, many people continue to live happy and healthy lives without money.

Doesn't it seem conflicting that some groups, past and present, have no money, no bombs, no crime, no poverty, no homelessness, no pollution, no debt, and live sustainable, healthy, and community-focused lives, and yet some of us would view them as primitive?

While we shouldn't over-romanticise earlier times, nor assume that they were without fault, we should remain open-minded to the idea that we could learn a great deal from those before us. We should shatter the illusion that mankind is always progressing in a positive linear fashion. If we take the Tsimané people–an indigenous hunter-gatherer and small-scale farming group in Bolivia–we can see that their way of life, similar to that of our ancestors, carries many health benefits lacking in the industrialised world. A recent study revealed that almost 90% of the Tsimané people had clear arteries, indicating a zero risk of heart disease[32]. In fact, they have the cleanest arteries of any population that has ever been studied. They also show extraordinary results for common Western disorders like insomnia, which is so rare in the Tsimané group that they don't even have a word for it in their language[33].

I am not suggesting we return to old ways. This movement is about doing the best we can with what we have and continuously striving to be the best versions of ourselves. It is about improving with stronger foundations and carefully considered incentives. Entrenched ideologies such as money shouldn't be free from our critique; we should actively question them. Where did money come from? What did we do before it?

## A Bite-sized History of Money

Before trade and money, people were a lot more self-sufficient and lived off the land as hunter-gatherers. The popular belief amongst anthropologists is that these groups maintained social and economic equality, with women having as much influence as men and no permanent leaders[34]. And their self-sufficiency awarded them great freedom.

"Hunter-gatherers had no money. Each band hunted, gathered and manufactured almost everything it required, from meat to medicine, from sandals to sorcery. Different band members may have specialised in different tasks, but they shared their goods and services through an economy of favours and obligations."

-Yuval Noah Harari

No one owned land. Land was just part of life, and it provided for the people, as it did for wildlife. It was impossible to distance oneself from natural resources as one had to constantly engage with the surrounding elements. If these early hunter-gatherers began to deplete the natural resources, they would be forced to explore new environments and adopt more sustainable practices.

Through the evolution of agriculture, technology, and language, people began to form more complicated societies. More specific roles within communities were created, but all the while a direct connection to natural resources was maintained.

As tribes grew, they began to trade amongst other communities. The items traded would include simple raw food items such as rice, barley, fish and salt. As technology developed further, people would begin to trade advanced hunting and farming equipment.

As cities started to develop, a key shift was made towards a detached, artificial representation of wealth. Sometime around 1000 BC, Chinese societies moved from trading real tools to exchanging miniature replicas of them. This facilitated transactions which could be settled at a later date. Due to practical reasons, the sharp edges of the miniature pitchforks, spades and spears were replaced for smoother, rounder objects which would eventually become coins.

Before this transition it would have been a lot harder to stockpile wealth. Instead, one would invest into their community and a sustainable relationship with the environment. As people transitioned away from natural resources, the idea of ownership was redefined.

A hunter-gatherer has and owns very little. They share and use what is available to them. In hunter-gatherer times a man or woman with one million fish could be viewed as clearly having a mental illness. After all, what would be the purpose or statement of such excess? Once the hunter-gatherer has fed themselves and their community, the fish will spoil, attract predators or restrict movability. It certainly wouldn't make sense for a hunter-gatherer to keep such excess while people in their community go without food. During this time an individual's success could be measured by their contribution to the community. On the other hand, someone with one million coins could become very powerful and have a wealth of opportunities presented to them. Money became the measurement of wealth, and it facilitated isolated power.

Various iterations of money evolved at different times in different places. Other forms of ancient currencies included stones, rings, feathers, shells and animal bones. There were also agreements such as clay tablets which served as tallies and IOUs. As money found its shape across the world, people sought to make it transportable, hard to copy, divisible, durable and ultimately privatised, controllable and powerful.

## Multiplying Middle Men

With the new-found ability to accumulate and stockpile wealth, rulers and businessmen could harvest power. Through new opportunities, we have been pushed further and further away from natural resources. In hunter-gatherer times, you would go and collect your food and would visibly see the source.

There is only one link in this chain between you and the item:

you ↔ source

With trading, the number of links began to grow:

you ↔ your item ↔ their item ↔ their source

With money this chain can grow exponentially further:

you ↔ your labour ↔ your money ↔ their item ↔ their labour ↔ their money ↔ their supplier ↔ their source

With a one-to-one exchange between you and the environment, you can clearly see your impact. With a few more links in the chain it is fairly simple to trace things back to the source. However, it is incredibly difficult to locate the resources that go into making modern products like smartphones and laptops. These items could include thousands of people, hundreds of components, and many countries from all around the world. The longer the chain–facilitated by the exchange of money, and driven by a desire for more money–the more opportunities there are for exploitation and corruption.

As we become increasingly detached from our environment, we are less aware of the practices behind our products. The more links in the chain, the less we know, and the less we feel empowered to change things.

In addition to this, one could also argue that modern corporations actively keep consumers in the dark. An example of this is the corporations who spent over $100 million to prevent the labelling of genetically modified ingredients[35]. Sadly this is not an isolated incident, as corporations frequently target influencers and policymakers to conceal profit-hindering information. This often results in those who are supposed to be protecting us becoming highly compromised as they are funded by those with a clear conflict of interest. An example of this is The American Society for Nutrition, whose list of sustaining members include: Coca-Cola, Mars, Monsanto, Nestlé, PepsiCo, and The Sugar Association[36]. We can also see that The American Cancer Society[37], The American Diabetes Association[38], and The American Heart Association[39] are all receiving vast sums of money from private pharmaceutical companies. In fact, the pharmaceutical industry consistently spends more money on lobbying than any other industry[40]. With such apparent conflicting interests and vast sums of capital, it's no wonder that the public are frequently unaware of the consequences of our lifestyles and products.

It is interesting to consider whether we would still purchase some of our items if every link in the production chain was openly provided to consumers:

· Would we eat unsustainable products if we saw that acres of rainforest had to be cleared every second?[41]

· Would we still buy palm oil if we personally had to set fire to the tree, inhabited by the last family of orangutans?[42]

· Would we still buy designer clothing if we could see the textile factories poisoning the rivers in Bangladesh and subsequently poisoning the local communities and wildlife?[43]

· Would we still buy smartphones if we saw the four-year-old children working in the harmful and unregulated cobalt mines of southern Africa?[44]

· And would we purchase coffee if we saw the child slave workers of the Ivory Coast?[45]

The unpleasant truth is that the clothes we are wearing, the food we are about to eat, and the items that fill our homes, are likely to carry some form of suffering. If you set out to live a healthy, fulfilling, sustainable and moral life, unfortunately you may well be swimming upstream.

In our current systems the recurring crimes are so jarring as they conflict with fundamental human values. It is a sad state of affairs when you can make a video of a current factory with no edits, narration or music, and when you show that video to someone they may cry, feel angry and incredibly misled. When the truth can hurt so deeply, we have to create a better truth.

Nobody wants to do unnecessary harm to others; however, the victims are often hidden from us. With regards to our current unsustainable practices, the biggest victims may have yet to be born. We know that our enjoyment of certain foods, luxuries and comforts shouldn't come at the expense of others. Consumers of such products are not bad people, they are simply unaware. Similarly, unethical corporations are not 'evil rulers' with Machiavellian intent. They are by-products of an unhealthy system. They efficiently follow blueprints for making money in a system that will consistently reward their actions.

It shouldn't be unreasonable to demand that our governments and corporations need to be fully transparent about resources and practices. Hiding these things only benefits those seeking private financial gain. This is not about telling people what to do, nor preaching. This is about being honest and transparent, and providing the people with the tools that they need to make decisions that are in line with their own personal values.

The ramifications of decoupling us and our natural resources cannot be overstated, as it is a key contributor to our current environmental crisis. We believed that we could own and exploit the planet. A new narrative moved us away from interconnection to a world where we could exploit people and natural resources in the quest for private wealth. We started to believe we no longer needed to act sustainably, and we no longer needed to protect and maintain clean water, clean soil and a clean atmosphere. We began to think as though we had evolved past nature. We began to fly over our oceans and trains could cut through our forests. We no longer needed the stars to navigate nor the wind to push our sails. We no longer needed the support of our communities as we could become individuals with access to a wider range of consumables. We sacrificed clean air for speed, clean soil for convenience, and clean water for comfort. We started to abuse our resources and our sustainable relationships. We built walls and cities which concealed the consequences. We moved from natural and sustainable living to an artificial, unsustainable story.

## Hidden Wealth

In modern times money is quickly losing its final link with a real-world resource as it is transitioning from metal coins and paper notes to digital binary values. Now more than 90% of all money is digital and exists only within computer servers[46]. One's wealth can be completely concealed from others, and purchases can be made with a discreet tap of a plastic card or the push of a button.

What does a hidden currency facilitate? To explore this, let's hypothetically create a new currency, purely as a visual device to gain another fresh perspective. This hypothetical currency is apples. Apples are earned or inherited the same way as modern money. The difference is that they cannot be concealed: they must be with you at all times. Let's also pretend that you can live a healthy life on an apple a day, and that the public only eat apples. To relate this to modern society, let's break down what people would look like in a city with this new visible currency:

· Some people might frantically search for discarded apple cores just to survive. This could represent a homeless person. They would have no visible apples.

· Some people would have enough for the week but be under immense stress and uncertainty, wondering when the next batch would arrive. This represents working people facing redundancies, health bills, car repairs, injuries and so on. These people could carry their apples in their hands.

· Some people would have a modest amount, perhaps enough for a month or two. This could represent those in a stable yet low-paying job. These people could carry their apples in transparent bags.

· A select few would have billions of apples. This represents a wealthy business person. They would be surrounded by huge towers upon towers of apples. Rather than being hidden in offshore accounts, these apples, as much as 114 billion*, would tower over the area. To put that in to perspective, if each apple was placed one on top of the other, it could reach the moon and back ten times over.

---

* Jeff Bezos has a reported $114 billion.

22

In this hypothetical situation would people act differently with the inequality being so visible? Would the wealthiest members of society be able to walk past those frantically scrambling for a single apple when they know that they have far more than they would ever need? Would you judge people more based on their contribution to society?

## The 'Game'

"Money is a scoreboard where you can rank how you're doing against other people."
-Mark Cuban

With a concealable digital currency, businessmen and women are less accountable for their actions. They can also emotionally remove themselves from the real impacts of inequality as overtly harmful business practices can become a seemingly victimless 'game':

· "Business is more exciting than any game."
-Kitty O'Neil Collins

· "Money was never a big motivation for me, except as a way to keep score."
-Donald Trump

· "You can manipulate consumers into wanting and therefore buying your products, it's a game."
-Lucy Hughes

And in the infamous words of the multibillionaire media mogul Ted Turner, a man who inherited his father's advertising company in his early twenties: "Life is a game. Money is how we keep score."[47]

In our current economic system many of us are born into families with no money and with many other disadvantages, such as mental and physical health issues, a lack of family or little-to-no education. On the other hand, there are others who are born with millions in the bank and many other advantages, such as health insurance and private education. This is unfair and unnecessary. The people who say that there is nothing wrong with this level of injustice, and that there is nothing that we can do about it, are often those greatly benefiting from the current inequality. The children of the world should not be born into a cruel and unjust lottery.

In order to emotionally cope with great inequality whilst still maintaining the advantages, the billionaires of the world often create false senses of justification. An example of this can be seen during a live interview with Donald Trump on the Today Show[48]. When asked if he had ever been told no, Trump–a man who was born into an incredibly wealthy family and inherited his father's business–replied, "My whole life has been a no and I fought through it ... it has not been easy for me ... my father gave me a small loan of one million dollars." Firstly, only mentioning a one-million-dollar loan while leaving out the fact that he later inherited a reported 40 to 200 million dollars is highly misleading[49]. Secondly, and perhaps more importantly, labelling a million dollars as a small amount clearly highlights his detachment from reality.

## The Root of All Evil

Without wanting to go too far down the rabbit hole, and certainly not wanting to enter the world of conspiracy theories, there are at least a few things that it is important to know about our modern monetary system:

Fiat Currency and Debt Money
A paper dollar bill would have previously represented a physical amount of gold. You could go in to the bank and receive gold in exchange for your paper bill. This is known as the gold standard. Today the American dollar,

like most major currencies, is a fiat currency. Fiat currency is money that is freely created by private banks rather than being backed by gold. It is then provided to governments and individuals as debt, and repaid with interest. This type of money now accounts for 97% of the economy[50].

The more fiat currency created, the more debt we will have. Recently the global debt reached a high of $225 trillion[51] and is set to reach an outstanding $1,140 trillion by 2050[52]. Debt is rapidly becoming the 'normal' state. Accordingly, Credit Suisse's Global Wealth Report revealed that if you have $10 and no debt, you have more wealth than 25% of Americans combined[53].

"Today there is more debt in the world than money."
-Jem Bendell

A privatised fiat currency and an ever-increasing debt creates a devastating ripple effect with many victims, including the environment. To catch up with a runaway target requires more products and services traded, resulting in an increased consumption of natural resources. However, as Jem Bendell, a leading figure in monetary studies, states, "We don't have an exponentially expanding planet ... and so this money system means that, for all our ingenuity, all we are doing is delaying the ultimate crash."[54]

"Profits mania is so deeply entrenched that we don't even realize how we're harming society."
-Paul Tudor Jones

In addition to the environmental consequences, it is important to consider how private fiat currency affects our democracy.

Money and debt greatly influence political decisions. Politicians may approve more infrastructure or enforce tighter austerity measures based on the amount of money in the economy. However, those in charge of money creation are unelected and compromised by private interests. Private banks control the amount of money in the economy. They can decide when to create it and they can negotiate their own terms. As money expert Ole Bjerg notes, "By privatizing our monetary system, and the creation of money, we have essentially handed over a very vital societal power to the financial sectors."[55]

"He who controls the money supply of a nation controls the nation."
-James A. Garfield

The Profit of War

It is difficult to deny that money has an influence on global warfare; at the very least due to the fact that there are many corporations* who continue to profit from it[56]. However, many theorists would argue that profit is often a leading reason to instigate modern warfare. An example of this is what is known as a 'commodity war', where a government will instigate a war to acquire profitable resources. Common examples of alleged commodity wars are:

· The Finnish-Soviet war, which was alleged to be over the control of nickel mining.

· The Pearl Harbour attack, which was alleged to be Japan's efforts to claim the resources of South Asia.

· The wars in Iraq and Libya, which were alleged to be attempts to control oil.

With the theories mentioned above, it is difficult to decipher fact from fiction. Perhaps we will never know the real motivations behind past wars. With Libya (which has the largest oil reserves in Africa) and Iraq (which has the fifth largest oil reserve in the world), perhaps stories are always going to be more tempting than the proposed humanitarian reasoning behind the conflicts. However, with recent email leaks, reports and confessions, we can at least see that there is often more going on than what we were previously told.

---

* General Dynamics, BAE Systems, Boeing, Lockheed Martin, and many others.

26

With regards to the Iraq War, the £13m *Chilcot Report*, an inquiry lasting seven years, revealed that Iraq posed no imminent threat. And recently, former UK Prime Minister Gordon Brown admitted that the war was "not justified."[57] And with regards to the war in Libya, the leaked Clinton emails also hint at ulterior motives behind the conflict. An email from Clinton's closest advisor, Sidney Blumenthal, revealed that the "humanitarian motive offered is limited, conditional and refers to a specific past situation."[58] This email was sent 11 days into the conflict; however, bombing continued for another 7 months.

While the humanitarian motives behind both of the wars are increasingly questioned, there is a unifying theory: the changing of currency. In October 2000 Iraq announced that it would be "dumping the U.S. Dollar–'the currency of the enemy'–for the more multilateral euro."[59] And before the war in Libya, Prime Minister Muammar Al-Gaddafi had plans to cease selling oil in U.S dollars and start a new African currency[60]. If Libya had succeeded in creating a unifying African economy backed by gold, it would have shifted the global economic balance. It would have empowered resource-rich African countries to negotiate new rates and rapidly grow their economies.

"I spent 33 years and 4 months in active military service, and during that period I spent most of my time as a high-class muscle man for Big Business, for Wall Street and the Bankers. In short, I was a racketeer, a gangster for capitalism ... War is a racket, it always has been, a few profit and the many pay. But there is a way to stop it ... It can be smashed effectively only by taking the profit out of war."
-Smedley Butler, U.S. Marine Corps General Major, two-time Medal of Honour recipient.

Echo of an Ignored S.O.S.
It is interesting to note that, throughout our history, many key figures have attempted to warn us about money and gold. In the King James Version of the Bible it reads, "For the love of money is the root of all evil."[61] Regardless

of your religious beliefs, looking at this quote solely as an ancient literary example, the author is clearly warning us about the lure of money.

In 1519 when the Spanish conquistadors invaded Mexico, the natives were very quick to notice that the newcomers were absolutely infatuated with gold[62]. When questioned on this obsession, conquistador Hernán Cortés replied, "I and my companions suffer from a disease of the heart which can be cured only with gold."[63] And in 1816, in a letter to John Taylor, Thomas Jefferson–founding father and U.S President–stated that "banking establishments are more dangerous than standing armies."[64] It appears that those before us were concerned with unhealthy obsessions, material possessions and that which can lead us astray from sustainability, community and democracy.

I do not believe money is the sole root of our problems. However, its origin and purpose are important in understanding current challenges. It is important to acknowledge that any system has consequences and that we can implement alternatives. Solely removing money from society will not be effective. We will have to create new systems with new goals and new purpose. We will explore these in greater detail in chapters to come.

You may wish to further explore the origins of money. You may explore the families involved in alleged banking cartels, such as the Rockefellers, Rothschilds, Morgans, Astors and Warburgs. You may even look at specific historical events such as the infamous Jekyll Island meeting and the creation of the Federal Reserve Bank. You may also explore ancient tablets or modern-day promissory notes. Through this continued research you will see that there are numerous debates as to whether money slowly evolved or if it was intentionally created and maintained as a tool of control. You are of course free to explore these areas as you wish, but please try to return to grounded, positive and actionable solutions to the problems that we face today.

# Success Sells

In our current system you can invest $10,000 in deeply immoral and unsustainable actions and be heavily financially rewarded. In contrast, you could spend the same $10,000 investing into compassionate, moral and sustainable actions and lose it all. We can see that positive actions don't necessarily help to increase your personal wealth. Why then, in the current system, is money regarded as a sign of success? A ruthless business figure could inherit and acquire a fortune and be praised as a brilliant business mind and viewed as a role model for society, even if their actions had a devastatingly negative impact on the environment and the quality of life of others.

When we see Top 100 rich lists there is no points system for whether their actions were for the greater good or if they were positively contributing to their community. A successful person could be someone who is kind, passionate, patient, scientific and caring. A successful person could be someone who is positively contributing and is living in harmony with their community and resources. Our systems could foster these kinds of people.

The evolution of money is much more than an economic transition. Understanding it also allows us to see the ideological shift that has taken place with regards to how we understand resources and ownership. We have come to see money as the main thing of value in society, rather than our labour, our communities, or our futures. The idea of private wealth has shaped how we coexist, how we communicate and how we view others.

It is interesting to hear from those who have experienced moneyless economies. They can offer authentic insight into the social changes mentioned above. Stephen Goldsmith is from the moneyless Australian aboriginal group Kaurna. When describing his moneyless culture he noted, "In our language we have no such word as please or thank you, because it is what is expected of us, that we share and give what we have … There was no such word as mine in my culture, it is ours, it is a collective, it belongs to all of us. [In modern times, with money and ownership] we don't share, we don't give. It kills us as human beings, as a society, as a race."[65]

## Owning the Land Beneath Your Feet

"History is important. If you don't know history it's as if you were born yesterday. And if you were born yesterday, anybody up there in a position of power can tell you anything."
-Howard Zinn

Modern English land division originated, in part, from the Norman invasion of England in 1066 C.E. The new monarchy audited the land, created new laws and enforced taxes, influenced by the infamous Domesday Book. The book was a survey of England, carried out by royal officers to help determine what dues were 'owed' to the new King. Essentially all land belonged to the self-elected ruler, William the Conqueror. Land was granted to lords who became landlords. England was divided into shires–geographic regions for administrative purposes–which are now known as counties. Many counties today, such as Hertfordshire, Lancashire, and Bedfordshire, still bear the suffix of shire.

The King's senior officers of the land, known as reeves, became managers of the people. These shire reeves–a term later shortened to sheriffs–were responsible for collecting royal revenue. The King ordered numerous castles to be built throughout the land to protect and control 'his' new kingdom. As a huge fan of hunting, he seized and depopulated great swaths of England, from which he created royal hunting grounds. An example of this is the New Forest in Hampshire, which was created at the expense of more than 20 hamlets and numerous agricultural plots[66]. The land became a royal forest and was used to hunt deer. To this day the New Forest is still largely 'owned' by the crown (roughly 90%)[67].

The King also introduced a new language to be used by the elites–Norman

French–which created a communication divide between the rulers and the general public. New terms, conditions, and ideologies were developed and enforced without full clarity. Throughout this period there were many rebellions by the natives, which resulted in further changes to the land by way of more castles and garrisons, which were accompanied by yet more enforcers.

The landlords would offer vast areas of the country to family and other elites. This new division of land created a complicated hierarchy of land ownership, with the king at the top, royal families, lords and elites in the middle, and paying tenants at the bottom. Rent was paid by way of personal service, produce, protection and money. No single person could ever fully own the land upon which they lived and worked. Only the Crown had this privilege.

Isn't it shocking that so much of this system, set-up by a power-hungry, unelected, invading king is still in place today? It is clear to see that this system of ownership was not founded on moral principles that benefit the people, so why can't we implement a new one? The danger of not knowing our own history is that we might assume that the systems we have in place were democratically created and thoughtfully honed through centuries of calculated trial and error, and constantly refined by a transparent goal of the collective good. Unfortunately, however, we are, as noted by historian Graham Hancock, "a species with amnesia."[68]

"Those who cannot remember the past are condemned to repeat it."
-George Santayana

While the system has of course changed since the 11th century, the apple hasn't fallen too far from the tree. Nearly 1000 years later, over a third of the land in the UK is owned by only 1,200 families that have descended from aristocracy[69]. In 2016 it was revealed that the 6th Duke of Westminster owned a land portfolio worth £9 billion[70]. The Ministry of Defence is the second largest landowner in Britain, owning more than 500,000 acres of land. Its property portfolio is around £20 billion; however, it was 'purchased' for around £3 billion, which was ultimately paid for by the people by way of taxation[71]. In the U.S., media moguls such as John Malone and Ted Turner are the modern-day elites, owning an astonishing 4.4 million acres of land. Alongside the Crown, other notable landowners include those who have inherited money and property from the cattle, lumber and fossil fuel industries.

"The difficulty lies, not in the new ideas, but in escaping from the old ones."
-John Maynard Keynes

We know that being ruled by kings, earls, lords and elites whom we didn't vote for is not democratic or moral, but have we removed it from our system? Just because we inherited flawed and ancient ways doesn't mean that we have to pass them on to our children. Or put another way, we are borrowing the environment from our children - how will we return it?

In the next chapter we will explore the impact of money as a motivator. Do you have to abide by the law if you are wealthy? Have there been scientific studies on the psychological impact of money? Are legacy tools and concepts holding us back?

CHAPTER 3

# MONEY MOTIVATION

What does money promote?

"Communities and families have always been based on belief in 'priceless' things, such as honour, loyalty, morality and love. These things lie outside the domain of the market, and they shouldn't be bought or sold for money ... Money has always tried to break through these barriers, like water seeping through the cracks in a dam. Parents have been reduced to selling some of their children into slavery in order to buy food for the others. Devout Christians have murdered, stolen and cheated–and later used their spoils to buy forgiveness from the Church. Ambitious knights auctioned their allegiance to the highest bidder, while securing the loyalty of their own followers by cash payments. Tribal lands were sold to foreigners from the other side of the world in order to purchase an entry ticket into the global economy."

-Yuval Noah Harari

Money could be viewed as the grease in the machine of capitalism. It can help drive things. But are we driving in the right direction?

# Misguided Motivation

## Cars

Cars have developed a great deal since Carl Benz took his three-wheeled, horseless carriage for a spin in 1885. One could argue that money has caused this rapid progression. The main focuses within automotive development have always been gadgets, looks and speed. Yet from a sustainability and equality perspective, the focus should be on affordability, durability and the use of sustainable fuels and production methods. In fact, if we were to really act for sustainability, would it not be better to stop making cars altogether and develop sustainable alternatives?

Newer 'intelligent cars' are proving to be intelligent at extracting money from the user. When a modern car breaks down you have to take it to a bespoke shop, who then plugs it into a bespoke computer that informs you how much money it will cost to repair. If the development of automobiles was truly seeking to be the best for the public, cars would be built in such a way that you could diagnose and repair them yourself. Cars could be built to last. And at the very least, their fuels could be sustainable. Current diesel cars have been proven to run on used vegetable oil–something that is thrown away by millions of restaurants every day. And electric vehicles have been shown to be a viable option as they can be powered by batteries which can store energy harvested from the sun. This promotes a question - where would we be today if we had previously asked our leading automotive engineers to focus on sustainable, healthy and ethical travel?

## Televisions

Many corporations aim to advance technology for the sake of capital and market control. An example of this would be the next development in televisions, 4K resolution.

At present, many consumers own high definition televisions (HD TVs), with a resolution of approximately 2000 by 1000 pixels[*]. Current HD TVs are over four times the resolution of our previously accepted international standards and yet the TV manufacturers are pushing for another leap in resolution.

Nearly all of the modern films we watch today at the cinema are around 2000 by 1000 pixels, almost identical to our current HD TVs. Modern films are viewed on 50-foot-plus screens at the cinema every day, all around the world, and few would complain about inferior resolution. Why would we need 4K resolution, nearly four times the resolution of professional cinemas, in our living rooms, on a TV that is about four foot wide? Surely we should focus on more durable TVs, ones that last longer, use less energy, and are made from more sustainable and ethically justifiable resources.

In order to see whether a consumer really notices the increased resolution, we screened HD and 4K content on a 26-foot screen using a 4K professional cinema projector in optimum conditions. As part of the test we invited directors of photography, camera operators, editors, directors, VFX artists, and image technicians. When we asked the viewers which they preferred and if they noticed any difference, they either said that both resolutions looked identical or that neither was better than the other.

Despite the fact that the public didn't ask for it and that they will not see a noticeable difference, they will be sold the higher resolution via intense marketing. Consumers will be convinced that they need to 'upgrade' their current TVs. Even though most modern feature films today are not being completed at a 4K resolution, there are still 4K TVs in the shops.

Making 4K TV programmes increases the costs and resources for camera manufacturers, camera operators, onset departments, editorial departments, media storage technicians, visual effects teams, and many others. Despite all of this wasted energy and resources and the fact that it will result in billions of film and TV equipment ending up in landfill sites, it is still happening.

Built-in Obsolescence

Certain products are built with the intention of becoming defective after the

---

[*] Pixels are the tiny blocks of illumination which make up the surface area of a screen.

warranty period to fuel another purchase. This is known as planned, or built-in, obsolescence.

One of the most infamous examples of built-in obsolescence is the lightbulb. When lightbulbs first became publicly available in the late 1800s, the providers installed and maintained the complete electrical system. Given that the early contracts made the corporations liable for replacements, it was in their best interests to create long-lasting and robust products. Evidence of this can be found in Livermore, California, where a lightbulb–first installed in 1901–is still shining bright today, over a century later[72].

However, as the market developed so, too, did the money-making opportunity to produce disposable bulbs that had to be regularly replaced. This resulted in the well documented Phoebus Cartel of the 1920s. The cartel was comprised of the top manufacturers, and they colluded to artificially reduce the lifetime of lightbulbs to around 1,000 hours[73].

As BBC reporter Adam Hadhazy reveals, the practice is unfortunately alive and well today: "Handsets often get discarded after a mere couple years' use. Screens or buttons break, batteries die, or their operating systems, apps, and so on can suddenly no longer be upgraded. Yet a solution is always near at hand: brand new handset models, pumped out every year or so and touted as 'the best ever'."[74] Accordingly, a recent study revealed, "the average person disposes their smartphone after 2.7 years, a service life barely longer than that of T-shirts or flip-flops."[75]

This profitable tactic is also prevalent in the world of MP3 players. They are often sealed with large quantities of glue, filled with bespoke parts, and accompanied by little-to-no documentation on how the item is made. They continue to decrease the number of possible hardware upgrades; therefore, if you need more storage on the device you'll need to purchase a whole new unit rather than just a new memory card.

Planned obsolescence was once labelled by right-wing media outlets as an anti-capitalist conspiracy theory, perhaps partly due to the fact that we would often dramatise the practice. It can be more exciting to imagine an 'evil' backlit villain, hardwiring a countdown-to-malfunction timer into a product, which is set for just after the warranty period expiration date. Often though, it is the more mundane case of allowing products to be fragile in certain areas, hard to repair, and regularly updated–such as a slight modification to a bespoke charger or adapter.

Laura Trucco, a Ph.D student of economics at Harvard University, recently followed her suspicions to see if previous iPhones become slower when Apple release a new model[76]. To test her theory she collected data on how often people search "iPhone slow", which revealed six distinct spikes between 2008 and 2014 when she ran the test. As predicted, these clear spikes correlate with new iPhone releases. Trucco also ran the same test looking for "Samsung Galaxy slow", but she didn't find any trends correlating to the launch of new Samsung devices. This actually further proves her theory. While Samsung make their own handsets, the operating system they use is developed by Google. However Apple, unlike many other providers, creates both the handset and their own operating system. Therefore, they have the means to launch a new phone while simultaneously changing how their current models operate.

Sadly there is increasing evidence that built-in obsolescence is on the rise. A recent report revealed that, despite technological 'advancements', the share of large household appliances that had to be replaced within the first five years is rising[77].

However, there is a silver lining; the public are becoming more aware of corporate tactics and are demanding better practices. In 2016, Global News revealed that a petition had "been signed by over 300,000 users urging Apple to extend the lifespan of their devices."[78]


Rights
While we may think of ourselves as rapid innovators, it can be argued that we are incredibly slow at making very important change. While it is fascinating to see how much technology has advanced over the past 30 or so years, is it the correct focus of our energy, or are there more pressing priorities?

Less than a hundred years ago, women were not allowed to vote in the majority of Western countries. Even after women fought for the right to vote, they were often subjected to further inequality, and still are today. It is tragic that in 2016 we celebrated our 'progressiveness' when America, the land of the 'free', announced they would legalise same-sex marriages. Equal rights for everyone regardless of their gender or sexual preference should not even be open to debate, but an inevitable right at birth. The fact that we have invented planes, cars, TVs, computers, and sent people into space before we give others basic human rights shows that money can be an awfully misguided motivator. It can distract us from what really matters.

"We now have so many ways to connect yet so little interaction, we have higher profits but lower morals, more technology but fewer solutions–it seems that with each step forward we take two steps back. We are clearly misguided by the wrong incentives."
-Freewords

One might say that it doesn't make sense how products that we regularly use contain non-recyclable packaging, unethical and harmful ingredients that are flown all around the world, and come from corporations that are unregulated, untaxed, unsustainable and so on. When we say that these short-sighted actions don't make sense, what we mean is that they don't make sense for us as a collective, on a finite planet where we think about the future, where we listen to science, and where we act with compassion. However, if the motivation is to make vast quantities of money as quickly as possible, regardless of the consequences, then these unsustainable and deeply immoral acts make a lot of business sense.

"Everything that we think is detrimental, someone is benefiting from it, that is why that spell continues to perpetuate."
-Russell Brand

# Wings Clipped

In addition to money motivation being misguided, it can also slowdown innovation through competition. Companies frequently copyright ideas for increased revenue streams or to block other companies that compete against private interests. In other words, someone can have an idea and own and control it. Here are some hypothetical examples to illustrate how the practice of copyrights and patents could be a disservice to the public:

Agriculture
A hypothetical mass agricultural firm create a new type of seed that doesn't need sunlight and produces two times the normal yield. This could greatly reduce poverty by empowering the public to grow their own food with minimal land. However, by enabling the public the corporate farmers could lose revenue. In this example the company could patent the seed and control its use.

Cars
A hypothetical car company could develop a new type of air bag that provides 100% protection for its users. Rather than share this idea and increase the safety for all drivers, they could protect the idea and use it as a Unique Selling Point (USP) for their company alone.

These examples demonstrate how money could block or stunt new developments where the public are the ones who lose out. It also reveals the de facto mentality of corporations: to increase corporate dependence and private ownership.

Those of you who have seen an episode of *Dragon's Den* or *Shark Tank*—TV programmes where inventors pitch ideas to wealthy investors–will be fully aware of a question that the investors always ask: "Do you own the idea?" These agreements can diminish our self-sufficiency and increase our perceived need for private corporations.

When Benjamin Franklin was offered a patent for one of his inventions, he declined it and stated, "We enjoy great advantages from the inventions of others, we should be glad of an opportunity to serve others by any invention of ours; and this we should do freely and generously."[79] Clearly our current system does not value collaboration, contribution and compassion as much as the scientist and founding father.

To give some more real-world examples, Monsanto, who holds around 1,700 patents[80], and controls as much as 90% of seed genetics[81], is part of 5 companies* who, since the mid-90s "have bought up more than 200 other companies ... to dominate our access to seeds."[82] In addition to this, they have the following clause on their website: "When farmers purchase a patented seed variety, they sign an agreement that they will not save and replant seeds."[83] Monsanto actively creates barriers to our self-sufficiency. They create ways to make us dependent on them. They are seeking to commodify and monopolise the raw ingredients of life.


# Fraud Funds


In a 2013 investigation, CBC Marketplace discovered that not only were car mechanics up-selling their customers, recommending them services that they didn't need and carrying out dangerous practices, but they were also not completing the work that customers paid for[84]. They used the customer's lack of knowledge and equipment against them. On three separate trips, a sample car shop charged customers for work that they didn't complete. This was proven by inspections that took place before and after the sessions and further confirmed via hidden cameras. In 100% of the cases the customers were exploited. One employee noted, "I'm not proud of it, but that's how we were taught ... you were forced to rip people off."

This was apparently done "because all the owner's looking for is money

---

* Monsanto, Syngenta, Bayer, Dow, and DuPont

[and] if he's not making money then you're no use to him." The promise of a financial pay-off outweighed an honest service to the public. Another employee confessed that the goal was "to sell as many services and get as big of a bill as you possibly could on every vehicle." When asked how often he committed fraudulent activities, he admitted that it occurred "multiple times a day." One ex-employee revealed that after questioning the immoral practices, the owner of the company told him to "go save the whales somewhere else [as] this is an up-sell world."

As the primary focus of a company is often to create money, what happens when customers don't need their services? What will happen if they are in financial difficulty and they are presented with the choice between moral actions and profitable actions?

In the case of the oil change investigation, they also discovered dangerous operations in which the company cut corners to reduce costs, sometimes putting the customers' lives at risk due to the distraction of increasing profit. While this example may seem like a small and self-contained incident, it is happening on a daily basis all over the world. Money-making opportunities put our lives in danger as safety checks are skipped, standards are loosened and cheaper materials are used, all in the pursuit of increasing profits. Below are some more examples taken from a recent report[85]:


· 4 million Fords were recalled due to faulty seat belts.
· 6 million GM vehicles were recalled due to sudden acceleration change.
· 7 million Toyotas were recalled due to faulty power.
· 7 million Fords were recalled due to ignition switch fires.
· 9 million Toyotas were recalled due to faulty pedals.
· 14 million Fords were recalled due to cruise-control switch fires.
· And 21 million Fords were recalled due to parking gear faults causing the car to roll.


What's more, U.S. auto recalls are on the rise.[86]

*Fake Britain* is a UK consumer rights programme that frequently exposes fraudulent activities conducted by those out to make money. So far, they have made over 100 episodes and each one exposes multiple companies and products, some of which include faulty smoke detectors, harmful shampoos, unlicensed landfill sites and a company who would target the elderly, make them afraid in their own home and then sell them overpriced key insurance.

While the programme does a fantastic job of revealing malpractices, it doesn't attack the root of the problem: a lack of corporate transparency and the reward of money. In the relentless pursuit of greater profits and more isolated power, large corporations will only continue to put our lives in danger. Rigorous testing, safety checks and consumer wellbeing can be viewed as inconvenient profit reducers that hinder capitalism's sacred incentive: money.

"Capitalism trades in futures."
-Terry Eagleton


In 2017, The Guardian revealed that Monsanto "continued to produce and sell toxic industrial chemicals known as PCBs for eight years after learning that they posed hazards to public health and the environment."[87] Therefore we have a company proven of consciously harming us in control of a large proportion of our food supply.

While corporate crimes such as those of Monsanto may appear worthy of a spy film super-villain, the consequences are painfully real. One could argue that money motivation can facilitate suffering, and that perhaps we currently live in an era where ethics can be viewed as too expensive.

Walmart, the world's largest brick-and-mortar retailer[88], is frequently involved in monetary scandals. As CBC News revealed, the retail giant has "$76 billion in assets through a network of undisclosed subsidiaries in 15 tax havens."[89] In addition to this, they were proven guilty of forcing employees to work through their lunch breaks. In the quest for more money, they encroached on the rights of their own employees. And even when proven guilty, the company dug its heels in and delayed repayments. Nearly 200,000 workers who have been waiting to get paid for ten years have only just received their paycheques[90].

The frequent cases of Walmart are even more disturbing when you look at the vast amount of money made by the Walton family, who own 55% of the company. As noted in Forbes, "six Waltons have more than the bottom 30% of Americans."[91] Walmart averages a profit of $1.8 million every hour[92]. Clearly it can pay to be unethical.

"There are companies that do good for communities, they produce services and goods that are of value and that make our lives better, and that's a good thing, the problem comes in the profit motivation, there's no such thing as enough."
-Michael Moore

# Too Big To Fail

One could still label the previously mentioned incidents as careless mistakes; however, I would argue that they are often highly calculated, intentional strategies. Large companies put aside huge sums of money to help pay their way out of immoral acts that they fully intend to carry out. Monetary fines and profitable fraud are viewed through a callous business lens. Corporations ask themselves whether the benefits of crimes outweigh the potential loss if they are caught. JP Morgan Chase, a global financial firm and one of the largest banking institutions in the U.S., are a clear example of a corporation which, one would assume, frequently poses such questions. Some of the JP Morgan Chase fines and settlements include:[93]

· $160,000 for inaccurate reporting.
· $500,000 for failing to disclose information.
· $1.5 million to settle a sex discrimination lawsuit.
· $100 million to settle a lawsuit for increasing minimum credit card payments.

- $153 million for misleading investments.
- $264 million for corrupt hiring practices.
- $270 million for mortgage misrepresentation.
- $389 million for illegal credit card practices.
- $400 million for breaking EU regulations.
- $920 million for trading fraud.
- $1.3 billion for currency manipulation.
- $5.1 billion for state and federal law infractions.
- $5.3 billion for foreclosure abuses.
- And $13 billion for a civil settlement for foul mortgage lending leading up to the 2008 financial crisis.

With such a high number of reported cases–of which there are more–one must wonder how much they get away with. And at this point, even if they get caught, are they now too big to fail? It seems that to JP Morgan Chase, with an elite and powerful network and over $2.4 trillion in assets, laws are no longer an insurmountable obstacle. Restrictions are not a deterrent as they can position themselves as such to be above the laws that most of us are bound by. In addition to this, they spend millions of dollars every year lobbying Congress for financial reform to shape the laws to fit their needs[94]. The motivation of power and profit is too strong for many in our current capitalist system. Many corporations are now above the law and can make their own rules.

"Power tends to corrupt, and absolute power corrupts absolutely."
-John Dalberg-Acton

Even if a company eventually falls due to fraudulent activities, those at the top will often escape very well compensated. Lou Pai, who was a key figure at Enron, left just before the company went down after multiple criminal investigations. He left with a private bounty of over $280 million, enabling him to purchase many extravagant properties, including a 77,500-acre ranch in southern Colorado complete with its own mountain; making him the second largest landowner of the entire state[95]. When Enron eventually went bankrupt, 20,000 employees lost their jobs and billions of dollars were lost in retirement, medical, and pension funds[96]. Meanwhile the top executives–who had previously cashed in over $100 million in stocks–were paid bonuses totalling $55 million. Enron is an example of a company too big to fail, even after they have fallen. And Lou Pai must have fallen from great heights, as he landed upon a mountain, which he now owns.

"Another way of saying too big to fail is that we have socialised the risk but privatised the reward."
-Mick Taylor

## Shaping Science

Corporations not only have the power to bypass democracy and create new laws, they can even shape science to achieve their private goals. Reports from the University of California showed that the sugar industry paid scientists to play down the link between sugar and heart disease[97]. And a recent New York Times article revealed that "Coca-Cola funds scientists who shift the blame for obesity away from bad diets."[98] In addition to this, many corporations directly target our hospitals, as the biggest pharmaceutical companies routinely pay doctors to promote their highly profitable products[99]. In a deadly two-pronged attack, corporations can shape modern science and even the application of it.

## Double Standards

If you have partaken in backcountry camping, you may be aware of the stringent rules that are in place. As they highly value sustainability, you could be breaking the law if you snap a single tree branch. This is interesting to consider as current unsustainable diets, promoted by Western governments, result in 1.5 acres of rainforest being destroyed every second[100]. Breaking a tree branch whilst camping doesn't impede private wealth and, therefore, considerate limits are enforced. Highly unsustainable and avoidable food practices on the other hand, are incredibly profitable and therefore no authentic limits are imposed. The policy makers claim to value sustainability but turn a blind eye to the worst offenders.

There is also a conflicting double standard forced upon wildlife. Deer populations are culled when they begin to approach an unsustainable rate of consumption, even though they are just consuming what they need to survive and know no alternative. However we, as a highly evolved species, are not only unnecessarily destroying acres of forest every second but we also frequently leave behind vast areas of barren wastelands. We hold animals to higher levels of sustainable rigour than businesses.

## Crazy Corporations

"The first industrial revolution is flawed, it is not working, it is unsustainable, it is the mistake, and we must move on."
-Ray Anderson

Dr. Robert Hare, consultant to the FBI, explains that if we look at corporations as people we can see that many of their traits could be classified as those of a psychopath[101]. This could include things such as cheating, lying, deceitfulness and knowingly harming others. In Mark Achbar and Jennifer Abbott's documentary, *The Corporation*, they expose Exxon, IBM, General Electric, Chevron, Kodak, Pfizer, Sears, Hyundai, Daewoo, Roche and countless others, as examples of corporations who have paid hundreds of millions in criminal, environmental and fraudulent fines, and yet still present themselves as 'good people'.

Money-motivated fraud creates a very defensive environment. You may find yourself constantly doubting the authenticity of your purchases as you know the motivation behind their creation may be misguided and not led by a genuine desire to best serve the public. Even if a company sells the image of compassion, you may be sceptical. Occasionally, you will witness windows into to what a more genuine world could look like. There may be times when you ask someone in a shop where to find a certain item, and in some cases they may recommend that you go elsewhere. These instances frequently appear when the employee isn't distracted by money, such as after they have handed in their notice. In this scenario the removal of money from the equation allows the person to act via their own morals and values, which can result in genuine service.

# Polluting Politics

In June 2017, the UK's Conservative Party were involved in a canvassing scandal. Channel 4 went undercover and released damning proof that the party had set up a secret call centre to canvass for votes before the upcoming general election[102]. The cold calls tended to promote the Conservative Party and its members whilst criticizing the leader of the opposition. The callers falsely claimed to be an independent market research team–this is a criminal offence. One of the directors of the operation, Sascha Lopez, was caught on camera directing his staff to lie to the public.

Millions of people around the UK are registered with the Telephone Preference Service (TPS). These households have chosen to opt out of nuisance calls. As Channel 4 reporter Ciaran Jenkins notes, "it is illegal to call them to promote anything, including political parties."[103] Despite this, those who had registered with TPS still received calls that were promoting the Conservative Party.

The party used their wealth to pay others to commit criminal acts on their behalf. Laws protecting privacy and democracy were broken. With these kinds of criminal tactics, one must wonder whether the number of funds is more important than policies when gaining votes. And are exposure, popularity and repetition more important than being accurate and ethical?

In an Independent article it was revealed that the "Conservatives raised more than 10 times as much money from large donors" when compared to their opponents. And in the final days leading up to the election they received "nearly £19,000 an hour."[104]

In addition to private funding, the media also has a huge influence on votes, and there was a heavy pro-conservative bias leading up to the UK general elections[105]. Perhaps this should come as no surprise as the UK press is largely owned by two pro-conservative billionaires: Rupert Murdoch and Lord Rothermere. The Conservatives went on to win the largest number of seats in a very close election with no majority rule.

## Money Motivation in Science

During a 2009 talk entitled *The Puzzle of Motivation*[106], Dan Pink presents numerous scientific studies which explore the motivation of money. One of these found that participants who worked with no reward were more efficient and faster at solving problems than those who were offered a financial reward. Dan Pink claims this is because the use of money as a motivator "dulls thinking and blocks creativity", and for some tasks these types of motivators "either don't work or, often, they do harm." He goes on to note that, "This is one of the most robust findings in social science." Accordingly, the London School of Economics reviewed over 50 studies and also concluded that financial incentives "can result in a negative impact on overall performance."[107] This was also echoed in the report *Large Stakes and Big Mistakes*, where researchers revealed that "higher incentives led to worse performance."[108]

Dan Pink concludes his presentation by revealing some more efficient and effective incentives that are superior to money: autonomy, mastery and purpose; in other words, the urge to direct our own lives, continued improvement and doing something in service of something larger than ourselves. These alternative incentives are echoed by leading psychologists Edward Deci and Richard Ryan, who proposed that people have three psychological needs: autonomy, competency and the feeling of relating to others[109]. We'll explore this in greater detail in later chapters, as these incentives are built into our hypothetical Free System alongside a new sustainable economy.

"The solution is not to do more of the wrong things, to entice people with a sweeter carrot, or threaten them with a sharper stick. We need a whole new approach."
-Dan Pink

## Money Minds

So far we have seen that money might not be the best motivator. It can promote and facilitate fraud and suffering. It can push people in the wrong direction and even halt positive progression. We have also seen that it can encroach on our freedom and even undermine our democracy. But does money change the way we actually think? Does it shape who we are?

Paul Piff, a leader in social psychology, conducted numerous experiments to decipher how money can change our personalities[110]. A simple example would be the experiment in which he used the board game Monopoly to simulate the effect of unfair advantages. In his experiment, two people play together. However, one randomly selected participant receives huge advantages, such as more moves, more money and other added bonuses. Inevitably, these unfair advantages enable them to win the game.

As the game started, the researchers noticed subtle differences between the players. This included minor signs of dominance from the 'wealthier' player, who would make more noise while moving their counter around the board.

As a side-experiment, researchers placed a bowl of pretzels on the table. They noted that even though the pretzels were freely available to both participants, the 'richer' players would consume more. They also noted that these players were frequently rude to those with 'less money'.

After the experiment, the researchers interviewed the participants. The winners, those who were given an unfair advantage at the beginning of the game, started to explain how they 'tactically won', and how they 'earned' their victory. The winners seemingly forgot that they were given an advantage. This could suggest that even those benefiting from it dislike the idea of unequal opportunity at a subconscious level.

In another experiment it was revealed that richer participants are also more likely to cheat, and more likely to take something, even after being informed that it was specifically reserved for someone else. Those who felt wealthier took twice as much[111].

"In surveys we've found that it's actually wealthier individuals who are more likely to moralize greed being good, and that the pursuit of self-interest is favourable and moral."
-Paul Piff

Piff's experiments also include studies done with real money. In one of these, participants are given $10. They are told they can donate as much or as little of it to someone else anonymously. The participants with a salary of $25,000 or less donated nearly 50% more than those who earned $150,000 and over.

In another experiment, he noted that drivers were far less likely to stop at a pedestrian crossing if they were driving a more expensive car. All of the drivers from their least expensive category stopped at the crossing, whereas nearly 50% of the drivers from the most expensive category refused to stop and broke the law.

"As a person's level of wealth increases, their feelings of compassion and

empathy go down, and their feelings of entitlement, of deservingness, and their ideology of self-interest increases."
-Paul Piff

Piff and his team have run numerous experiments with thousands of participants and they continue to find trends. The wealthier participants are more likely to steal, to bribe, to lie and to endorse unethical behaviour. Piff doesn't report that less wealthy people are without flaws, he merely states that through his scientific research he has found that "the wealthier you are the more likely you are to pursue a vision of personal success, of achievement and accomplishment to the detriment of others."

We have always been surrounded by physical limitations: how fast we can run, how hard we can hit and how tall we can grow. And to a certain degree that keeps us in all in the same ballpark. However, with a form of stockpileable power, select individuals can tower above those around them.

It is healthy to be in a community with a strong sense of connection and contribution where we can view others as equals. There appears to be a narrow band of tolerance where certain hierarchies can sustain themselves. However, once an individual achieves a certain amount of isolated power, mental health issues can perpetuate. They can lose touch with those around them. Their thought processes can alter. Their morals and values can shift. Power can corrupt.

The old saying goes that if all you have is a hammer, everything can begin to look like a nail. Perhaps if individuals gain vast amounts of isolated power, everyone can begin to look inferior, or perhaps less-human, weaker, less worthy or even more controllable.


## Money Momentum


People are born with the ability to do many things. Our environments can shape our actions and bring out certain qualities. Money is part of a complicated system and it can facilitate harmful practices. While I may criticise the actions of corporations such as Monsanto, Apple or Nestlé, I am not suggesting that they are evil 'people' tainting a fair and sustainable system. When they sign a contract that harms others, I don't think that they are doing it because they want to cause pain, but rather because they view it as a victimless game, a number on a spreadsheet. The decisions are not viewed through an ethical filter. They are based on if a number goes up or down. This is particularly the case when you consider the global stock market, where middlemen can trade representations of representations. It becomes second nature to remove themselves from external consequences. They feel entitled by the right to consume and the right to accumulate unlimited wealth. They can remain hidden from harsh truths. Money can become the primary focus.

"The traders who are involved in the market do not have a moral fibre when it comes to environmental conditions, they're not rattled at all, they're just seeing dollars."
-Carlton Brown

As Elon Musk states, "Economics 101: What you incentivise will happen."[112] Unfortunately, our current systems can incentivise exploiting people and the planet, in so far as it can financially reward those actions. If you can pay little to no tax, if you can get away with polluting the planet, using harmful and unsustainable components, and if you can pay your employees the bare minimum, then you can make personal gains.

We can be incentivised to allow problems to grow as ignoring consequences can be highly profitable. Manufacturers can profit from unregulated factories in economically challenged areas, pharmaceutical companies can profit from a lack of preventive measures, private prisons can profit from a lack of rehabilitation, and online gambling companies can profit from pain and isolation.

As more ingredients for life become commodified and the rewards of wealth grow, there is even more incentive to increase capital. And there is no limit as corporations can continuously stockpile wealth. The more money they have, the more opportunities and power they can gain. They can reach a level where the law doesn't apply. They can create monopolies and shape the system to harvest greater control. They can remove boundaries, rewrite regulations, and even manipulate and shape science. Money can flow upwards.

It can become a self-perpetuating wrecking ball. It starts as an innocent snowball tumbling down a mountain. With each roll it gets bigger. It continues to grow and gain momentum. The core strengthens and solidifies. With each turn it is rewarded with more power and stability. It can become uncontrollable. It can move at such speeds that its perspective is no longer relative to those around it. It can break down barriers. It can destroy resources. It can become unsustainable and harmful.

We could try to catch these things sooner. We could increase legislation. We could try to build more barriers. But what if there was no snow in the first place? Could we replace a tool that is thousands of years old? Is it time for a new system? Could we be happier, healthier and more sustainable?

Before we explore potential solutions we must also explore the origins and consequences of consumer culture. While the facts may be hard to face, it would be irresponsible to ignore them. It would also hinder our ability to create a highly considered and preventative alternative.

## CHAPTER 4

# CHASING CONSUMERISM

Is consumerism healthy?

"Americanism: Using money you haven't earned to buy things you don't need to impress people you don't like."
-Robert Quillen

In Western Europe, at the start of the 18th century, economies boomed and wages began to rise. Centuries of ruthless colonising enabled select nations to purchase more luxury items–wants rather than needs. This facilitated our modern economic cycle. The more the public spend, the more companies produce. Labour increases, which in turn creates more income, and therefore more consumption. By the mid-18th century, the new economy was firmly established through an increasing array of products. Building on this momentum to further increase consumption, various advertising platforms were created and product rotations were introduced. This was a multi-pronged attack to promote spending well beyond one's needs.

Consumerism and the resulting societal changes were critiqued by many early philosophers who claimed it as vanity, which was seen as a sin. They feared that we would become slaves to luxury and idle consumerism. Swiss philosopher Jean-Jacques Rousseau called for a simpler way of life, large taxes upon luxury items, and a redirection of focus and energy towards nonmaterialistic values[113]. Rousseau's criticism, even at the very early stages of consumerism, triggered the debate between virtue and 'wealth' which continues to this day.

"Comradeship, dignity, amorosity, love, solidarity, fraternity, friendship, ethics: all these names stand in contrast to the commodified, monetised relations of capitalism."
-John Holloway

## The Rise of Commodities

By the mid-19th century, numerous locations were transitioning from agrarian societies* to industrial ones. Through the pursuit of wealth from materialistic items we developed new technologies and rebuilt our landscapes. We began to use more fossil fuels and redefined our societies through new social dynamics and class structures. Coal mines and factories replaced homes and fields as the new places of work. A key catalyst behind this transition was the development of the assembly line, where the creation of a product is broken down into many menial tasks to be quickly completed by hundreds of people in large factories. Karl Marx, philosopher and journalist of the time, believed this new system could repress the masses. He stated that under capitalism, man "becomes an appendage of the machine" repressed into "instruments of labour, more or less expensive to use, according to their age and sex."[114]

"Commodity producers do not appear as personalities with a determined place in the production process, but as proprietors and owners of things."
-Isaak I. Rubin

The capabilities and opportunities seemed to originate from the item or

---

* Agrarian societies are those that cultivate the land.

55

corporate brand rather than a known worker–this change in perception is known as commodity fetishism. Before this era we were more self-sufficient and maintained personal relationships with our community providers. We could name the creator - we could say, "I am going to get some bread from Mr. Jones as he is a very talented baker." Now, however, as our relationship with the maker is declining, we say, "The new iPhone is a must-have" without a single mention of who built the device. We begin to stop asking questions such as how was it made, as the corporation made it and its practices are trade secrets.

## Analysing Advertising

As production expanded, so too did our cities where large supermarkets created a false sense of self-sufficiency. An even greater array of corporations and products emerged, all fighting it out over the highly prized destination of our shopping carts. In modern-day supermarkets there can be hundreds of variations on a single product, all claiming to be the 'best'. We therefore confine our naturally inquisitive filter to limited scopes such as size, price and brand reputation. With so much to choose from, new corporate roles and strategies are continuously developed to ensure that the consumer chooses their product over those of competitors.

"On every street corner we are baited to booze, binge, borrow, buy, toil, stress, and swindle."
-Rutger Bregman

We are targeted by corporations at every stage of our lives. Even before we are born, we are affected by advertisements. A new mother's maternal instincts are used against them with marketing lines such as, "Ensure normal development" and "Protect your baby." These tactics are used to sell them all manner of things that, in reality, they don't need. Once the child is old enough to accompany their parents to the supermarkets, they will be greeted by their favourite cartoon characters on brightly coloured packaging.

Childhood idols are also used in TV commercials. During the 60s, a time when a lot of children were fixated on the moon landing, Cheerios used the following lines to introduce their cereal commercial: "Here's a team of junior spacemen with an out-of-this-world breakfast." Children are incredibly impressionable and susceptible to advertising as they quickly absorb and retain new information. In fact, it has even been shown that in many cases parental advice has not been able to reverse the impact of advertising[115].

This is a particularly troubling thought when you consider that children spend around 32 hours a week in front of a television[116]. Corporate entities are fully aware of the vulnerabilities of our children and frequently target them. Lucy Hughes, vice president at Initiative Media and the co-creator of *The Nag Factor*, openly promotes the strategic advantages of targeting children. She states that, "Anywhere from 20-40% of purchases would not have occurred unless the child had nagged their parents."[117] Promoting nagging is clearly detrimental to the relationships within a household as it actively shapes family interactions. When asked if her methods were ethical, she replied, "I don't know, but our role at Initiative is to move products."

In addition to manipulative product packaging and TV advertisements, corporations continue to find more efficient ways to target our children; one of which is through online games known as advergames. An advergame can appear as a harmless adventure game; however, it is built entirely around branded products. In 2012 scientists revealed that advergames can "persuade on a subconscious, emotional level", altering "children's behaviour without their conscious awareness."[118] They also revealed that "children as old as 15 do not recognise that advergames are adverts."[119] We have an increasing amount of screens between us, and often hidden on 'the other side' of that screen is someone seeking money.

Imagine if corporations had to advertise honestly, face-to-face. What would child advertisement look like?

You hear a knock at your door. It's a man who wants to speak directly to your children without you being present. You ask him who he works for, and he replies, "A powerful, tax-avoiding, unethical, unsustainable, multinational corporation." You ask him what he wants to say to your children, to which he replies, "I'd like to try to persuade them to desire expensive material possessions and highly addictive carcinogenic diets." He also adds, "I'll try to use their favourite cartoon character or computer game to lure them in, then I'll actively try to create friction in the family as it is known to move products." You close the door and 'politely' ask him to never return. Unfortunately, today's corporations find ways to go around the 'inconvenient barrier' of parental protection.

It seems that advertising campaigns will target us for our entire lives. In fact, even those no longer with us are not free from exploitation. A recent example of this would be the world's largest telecommunications company AT&T, who in a 9/11 tribute tweet included blatant product placement alongside a commemorative image of the twin towers[120]. They are not alone either, with companies such as Walmart[121], CVS Pharmacy[122] and McDonald's[123] all cashing in on the tragic event through tactless campaigns and marketing stunts. Lest we forget, Miracle Mattress and their infamous Twin Towers Sale[124].

Michael Pollan, renowned professor and nutrition expert, once stated that the only rule to defeat the way food advertising manipulates us is to avoid foods that have been advertised on television[125]. Although this may appear as a comedic comment he does go on to justify the health benefits of implementing this rule by stating that about 80% of this food is highly processed, and real foods don't have the budgets to advertise[126].

Aside from the negative effects of advertising, it's interesting to think about its very purpose. Commercials are ultimately there to sell products, which suggests the idea that, without the commercial, perhaps we wouldn't buy the product. This then poses the question: if it has a commercial, generally speaking, is it something that you don't need?

"For every pound earned by advertising executives, they destroy an equivalent of £7 in the form of stress, overconsumption, pollution, and debt; conversely, each pound paid to a trash collector creates an equivalent of £12 in terms of health and sustainability."

-Rutger Bregman

# False Advertising

Misleading and false advertising is all around us. A very common example is the money exchange sector. Firms will often use misleading terms such as 0% commission, implying that the customer is getting the best deal with no extra fees. However, while they may not be charging commission, they may well be offering a very poor exchange rate that they themselves define.

As an example, let's suppose you are converting 1000 Canadian Dollars (CAD) into US Dollars (USD):

A: An honest shop advertises a 2% commission charge in the shop window. They then apply the genuine market exchange rate of 0.9 (for example). Therefore, your 1000 CAD would become 900 USD. They then subtract the advertised 2% commission and so you walk away with 880 USD.

B: A dishonest shop advertises 0% commission in the shop window. They then apply their own exchange rate of 0.8. Therefore your 1000 CAD becomes 800 USD.

Even though example B doesn't apply an 'additional' commission fee, you still walk away with $80 less. If you are pressed for time and you see two exchange shops, one advertising 0% commission and another advertising 2% commission, you would likely choose the 0% option. You would trust that they are being honest, and you would lose money. They can earn more revenue and be financially rewarded for their lack of clarity.

Another example can be found in the highly competitive market of mobile phone contracts, where you are offered 'free' text messages, 'free' voicemails, and even 'free' phones–none of which are available unless you pay money and sign a contract.

Artificial services and job roles are frequently created to then be removed or reduced to appear as though you are getting a better deal. A fitness gym may remove the 'sign-up fee' if you sign up for an extra three months. And an estate agent may give you a 50% discount on the 'set-up and cleaning fees' before you move into your new apartment. These disingenuous services make you feel as though the company are helping you, when in reality they are exploiting your trust.

"We have put so much emphasis on profits, on short-term quarterly earnings and share prices, at the exclusion of all else. It's like we've ripped the humanity out of our companies."
-Paul Tudor Jones

## Image Manipulation

As many corporations are not motivated by our best interests and frequently target and feed our insecurities, it's no surprise that the images we see in the media are heavily manipulated. As media theorist Roy Thompson states, "What happens in actual reality has no bearing on screen reality."[127]

To give a very simple example, 14 is the average dress size in the UK, however the average size of a Hollywood actress is 4 to 6 (in UK sizes)[128]. Does this inconsistency between the real world and representations appear as identifiable differences or is there, as noted by French philosopher Jean Baudrillard, a dissolution of TV into life and life into TV?[129] When viewing a disproportionate average, are we completely aware of image manipulation or do we perceive it as reality? Do we act upon misinformed information?

Renowned molecular biologist Dr John Medina states that we "experience our visual environment as a fully analysed opinion"[130]; we instinctively compare what we see to our surroundings. And as professors Nikos Salingaros and Kenneth Masden note, we crave physical and biological connection to this visual analysis[131]. We instinctively try to fit in with the patterns that we create subconsciously. As such, viewing an inaccurate representation or a distorted reality can cause our brains to react upon misinformed information.

The brain has evolved to be highly efficient at grouping data and finding patterns, with or without our conscious involvement. Therefore when average-sized women see images with dramatically lower-sized models, it could indeed be harmful. As leading psychologist Helga Dittmar explains, "Ultra-thin media models cause body anxiety in vulnerable women through making salient discrepancies between their own body and weight."[132] This issue is not gender-specific but, as mentioned before, a neurological instinct. Accordingly, Dittmar also found the effects with men, where "idealised muscular media models cause greater body anxiety."[133]

The creation of body ideals portrayed by corporations can perpetuate mental health issues such as the development of anorexia nervosa: the act of self-starvation caused by a fear of weight gain. This fear can be caused through an inaccurate perception of the self. An underweight person suffering from anorexia sees an overweight person in the mirror. Their perception of their own reality has been altered. Image manipulation can have dangerous consequences as it can distance us from reality. It can make us feel inadequate, abnormal and alone.

As images become a larger part of our lives through portable technology, it is often easy to forget that they may have been carefully constructed and highly manipulated. When we see an advert for an anti-ageing cream, there is no clear caption or health warning below that states: "This woman is only 30 years old, although dressed in clothes that make her appear a lot older. She has been selected for her uncommonly smooth skin. We have applied heavy makeup and carefully directed lighting to create an even complexion. In addition to this, we have used computer software to digitally remove any signs of wrinkles, pimples, or anything that goes against the idea our brand is trying to portray." These hidden truths enable corporations to sell a lie, thereby enabling them to make more money as we might instinctively strive to comply.

As we are pushed towards digital perfection, our target is often not biologically achievable. Accordingly, cosmetic surgery rates have skyrocketed in the last decade[134]. A plastic surgery advertising campaign by Clinica Dempere uses the tagline, "We make fairy tales come true", and their billboards depict busty or chiselled, Disney-esque characters. Their campaigns highlight the fact that our new goals are often far from reality.

While some companies seem to promote the idea of leaving reality behind, many try to disguise the artificialness, often through the use of natural or supportive words. One common example is the Mommy Makeover, an operation designed to remove the naturally occurring body fat from post-birth mothers. The term Mommy Makeover makes it seem as though they are supporting mothers, when in fact they are creating and targeting their insecurities.

The goal of a plastic surgeon is usually individual financial gain and not a genuine desire to help the community. This can lead to excessive body modifications as many people are persuaded by an ever-evolving vision of perfection. Subjected people often develop body dysmorphic disorder (BDD) and are prone to plastic surgery addiction.

While many people cannot afford physical surgery, they can easily take part in a form of digital 'surgery' by carefully selecting and digitally modifying their social media profile pictures. This can in turn create further social anxieties around real-world interactions due to the fear of being 'discovered'. To preserve your artificial online portrait, you may hide your unfiltered and imperfect natural self from the real world.

A consequence of becoming isolated yet surrounded by images is a suppression of addiction and a growing feeling of shame. Many can feel confused, lost, or in pain and yet in the images they see it appears as though others are always 'living the dream' without even so much as a minor skin imperfection. The beauty of meaningful, real-world connections is that we can lower our guards and speak the truth. We all, at times, muddle through parts of life, and make it up as we go along. However, we are no longer comparing notes. Increasingly we suffer in silence. We are no longer communicating effectively nor seeing how similar we are. Rather than being truly present in the moment and creating authentic human connections, we can find ourselves reacting to a series of pop-ups and suggested links while scrolling down an endless digital page. We once adapted to nature, now we are increasingly adapting to technology and a culture of distractions and anxiety.

Pain can be a biological signal that things need to change. It can warn us that our current environment is unhealthy. However, it is all too easy to subdue said pain with a temporary high. Therefore yet another message can be lost in translation.

## Excess

"Money cannot buy peace of mind. It cannot heal ruptured relationships, or build meaning into a life that has none."
-Richard M. DeVos

Throughout our lives we have been pushed to consume. Our modern economic system has been built upon this very concept. Our increased distance from the natural world, then the item maker, and the way in which commodities are made and sold to us, all have complicated and often negative side-effects. In addition to this, the intense focus on the commodity itself also creates issues as we begin to lose connections with people and start to focus on material possessions.

"The things you own end up owning you."
-Chuck Palahniuk

Many can lose contact with the real world and fixate on money and commodity-related goals. This can happen to us all in varying degrees. And it can become a self-perpetuating mental illness. We can end up chasing an ever-moving target in the hope of a grounded purpose that we may be inadvertently running away from. There is no point where you are content when the target is excess.

"Money has never made man happy, nor will it, there is nothing in its nature to produce happiness. The more of it one has the more one wants."
-Benjamin Franklin

Celine Dion, a popular Canadian singer, has over 10,000 pairs of shoes[135] and yet there are millions of people in desperate need of a single pair. The Sultan of Brunei, Hassanal Bolkiah, owns over 7,000 luxury cars[136] and yet a single modest vehicle could drastically help someone in need. These are examples of when artificial, individual wants are in conflict with community. Every item is made from raw materials found on Earth. These raw items belong to no one person and therefore could be ethically and sustainably managed.

I don't mean to vilify pop singers nor wealthy people in general, but I wish to highlight the detachment we see when people drift away from human connection. We may not need to live in a world where in order to own two pairs of shoes, everyone would need to have at least one pair, but we should be conscious of those around us and the consequences of our actions. There are people with more than they would ever need while others are lacking the basic ingredients of life. On a finite planet with limited resources, can excess for a few mean stealing from the rest?

## Loss of Power

"The production of too many useful things results in too many useless

people."
-Karl Marx

Through the advent of online shopping, we have further lost our connection to resources and skills. Corporations and technology increasingly become the providers of life. This sense of dependence is further created though the rising culture of disposable consumerism, which affects not just environmental sustainability but our own independence. Subsequently, it becomes more difficult to imagine a scenario where you can opt out of the current system. And if we continue on this trend we may become fully reliant on new technology and a handful of multinational conglomerate businesses.

As disposable consumerism evolves we become replaceable units of an economy rather than valued members of a community. We are drifting further and further from authentic connection. And with the addition of a rising unregulated gig economy, an increasing amount of workers can also be viewed as a disposable commodity.

During this time of rising disempowerment, giant corporations can create the illusion of choice through a network of sister companies and product monopolies. This is visible in a haunting graphic released by Oxfam which depicts a tree of hundreds of recognisable food and drink brands with just ten companies at the top who own them all[137].

"There is no piece of legislation which is saying let's rein in the power of global capitalism."
-Brad Evans

We begin to feel as though we have lost the power to change things on a global scale. Accordingly, many begin to bury their emotions. Media theorist Mike Wayne states that, "Like all repressions this stems from not wanting to acknowledge something that hurts [and under capitalism there is a repression of] something that questions the very basis of your existence and your values."[138] We know deep down that the current system is failing us; we know that it isn't right. We know that companies shouldn't be allowed to target our children for profit. We know that there is inequality and unsustainable processes throughout our system. We know people are suffering. And we know even our own actions are likely to be perpetuating the problem.

## Consumer Culture

Within disposable consumerism, we can see the increasing commodification of cultural events. Christmas, Birthdays, Easter, Valentine's Day and weddings become less about human connection and celebration than consumption. Thanksgiving, one of the few remaining non-gift-based public holidays has become one of the most lucrative times to sell televised commercial space, as the whole family will be at home. Thanksgiving was supposed to be about giving thanks for the harvest and being grateful for what you have, a sentiment that is quickly washed away by the cultural events that now follow: Black Friday and Cyber Monday–the biggest days for discounted sales. Even if unaware of the contradiction of being immediately after Thanksgiving, we can still see that the images of Black Friday are hard to watch. When we see herds of people scrambling over one another and fighting over discounted material possessions, we can feel something is deeply wrong.

## Prisoners of Comfort

In an era with an increasing array of consumables we can, in many ways, become prisoners of comfort. However, in a more literal sense, the workers behind such commodities can indeed become imprisoned. A horrifying example of one of these prison-esque environments is the iPhone factory. In this giant dystopian workplace there have been frequent accusations of forced overworking to the point of collapse[139]. In fact, the conditions are so abysmal

66

they reportedly fitted safety nets to the stairwells to prevent suicide attempts[140]. Unfortunately, it is all too easy to conceal malpractices, especially when the workers are heavily monitored, not just on the production line but also in their sleeping quarters.

One way that the exploited workers of the world can expose the crimes against humanity is through the commodities themselves. An example would be the SOS letter that was found inside a Halloween decoration bought from Kmart[141]. The letter was written by a worker of the infamous Masanjia Labor Camp, where in addition to being held captive, forced to work long hours and victim to verbal abuse, the worker was also repeatedly physically tortured.

There was also the case of secret messages that were sewn into clothing bought from Primark which read, "Forced to work exhausting hours" and "Degrading sweatshop conditions."[142] And, very recently, shoppers discovered pleas for help sewn into clothing sold by retailer Zara, where workers revealed that their work went unpaid[143]. With such tightly monitored factories, it makes you wonder how many messages are left unseen. The true cost of many commodities is yet to be discovered.

## Valued Virtues

"Money is so central in our lives because it now embodies most clearly the central problem of man's life on earth–the dominance of the principle of personal gain. The great teachers of the world have always spoken of this as man's main weakness."
-Jacob Needleman

Throughout history, philosophers from all corners of the globe have warned us of deadly sins such as gluttony, envy, vanity and greed. These were known to corrupt, cause suffering, isolate power and dismantle communities. The same deadly sins seem to be the primary drivers of modern consumer culture. Our current system also seems to conflict with formerly highly valued virtues such as respect, charity, compassion and moderation. These were once seen as vital attributes to help create and maintain strong and healthy communities.

We are experiencing a commodification of virtues. We frequently value personal financial gain and opportunities over what is of value to those around us and our environment. Do we now value money over humanity?

We can face the facts with confidence as we also have the power to incite change–which we will explore very soon. First, we still have a couple of stones left unturned. In order to authentically design a better system we need to understand where we are at today. What is our current system? Is it democratic? It's time to peek behind the curtains and see what modern-day politics has become.

# CHAPTER 5

# BETWEEN TWO EVILS

What is modern politics?

O nce upon a time, you could work 40 hours a week and own a home. You could have free education and free health care. While one person was at work the other could raise the children. There was also a period of your life known as retirement, which began in your 60s. Even this humble scenario now seems like a wishful dream slipping through our fingertips.

It appears that we are subject to the cruel tides of capitalism. One generation may be able to afford a house where they grew up, the next may be priced out of the market. One generation may be able to afford health care, the next, perhaps not so fortunate. On these turbulent seas it does pose the question, are those at the top the captains of our titanic or the icebergs?

When we vote are we limited to one of two unauthentic 'solutions'? Do we view our democratic vote as damage limitation rather than a chance for genuine progressive change?

"You can almost not fix anything else until you fix the situation regarding money in American politics."

-Jane Mayer

# The Loudest Voices Are the Choices

On the 9<sup>th</sup> of November 2016, the world watched in shock as America chose a multi-billionaire businessman as their president-elect. A racist[144], sexist[145], lying[146], tax-dodging[147], over-privileged businessman who openly denies climate change[148] and said that Mexicans are rapists[149]. This man was voted for by over 60 million people and gained 306 electoral votes.

The opposition to Trump seemed to many like the choice of sanity, a dedicated and highly experienced candidate with the added potential of becoming America's first female president–a seemingly progressive message during troubling times. So why would people nominate Donald Trump over Hillary Clinton? How did the so-called most qualified candidate of all time lose against the so-called least qualified candidate of all time?

Hillary Clinton flip-flops on important moral issues. She was formerly against same-sex marriages[150], she voted for the Iraq war[151], she was under FBI investigation[152], she has taken the most money from lobbyists[153], she has been involved in several political scandals[154], she has been frequently caught lying with zero accountability[155], and she is funded by compromised corporations, corrupt bankers and 9 out of the 10 largest arms manufacturers in the world[156]. As John Pilger stated, "she is clearly the embodiment of a corrupt system."[157] While she may not be as openly brash, flippant and hateful as Donald John Trump, she is another portrayal of untrustworthy and corrupt politicians. As a former First Lady and Secretary of State, she represented the notion of maintaining current malpractices. Hillary became the vote for 'business as usual'. To many, voting for her was the progressive option, but to others it was a statement that you are satisfied with current operations and an unsustainable, unethical and dangerous system.

When viewing the world's current political systems, we can see that there is plenty of room for improvement. There is harrowing inequality, mass hunger and poverty. We are destroying our natural resources, we are losing our sense of community, we value possessions and we reward greed. Companies and politicians are seemingly above the law and a huge percentage of the population feel totally unrepresented.

When looking specifically at the U.S., we can see that it is one of the world's largest polluters[158], it has the highest number of prisoners[159], it is home to some of the most prolific corporate tax avoiders[160], it exports the most weapons[161], it spends more on warfare than any other country[162], it has the most expensive health care[163], it is currently bombing seven countries[164], it consumes the most calories[165], it has the highest levels of inequality in the industrial world[166], and if the whole world consumed as much as the average American we would need five planet Earths[167]. It is undeniably apparent that America, like many other countries, needs immediate, drastic and authentic change. As Hillary Clinton represented the current system, the option for an alternative rested with Donald Trump.

While an over-privileged billionaire is clearly not a representative of the people, Trump is, to many, a complete break from a conventional politician. He intelligently marketed himself as anti-establishment and vowed to clean up corrupt politics. To a country in desperate need of extreme change he could appeal to those eager for a new direction.

"It is hard to warn a population that Donald Trump is a dreadful solution when many people feel that their current situation is already a dreadful one."
-Russell Brand

As Trump himself once said, "You're living in poverty, what the hell do you have to lose?"[168] Trump is the equivalent of throwing an unpredictable change grenade into the old and tired barracks of the White House. Many of his supporters prayed that he would save the sacred trinity of the Senate, the Presidency and the House of Representatives, ridding them of their devilish corruption.

The very fact that people were willing to look beyond Trump's abundant flaws is a clear sign of system failure. People were prepared to vote against their own interests if it meant some form of transition from political trends. Trump is the result of trying to use a corrupt and broken system to fix what it has caused and/or maintained. The system puts forward those who can afford to play, and in an extortionate campaign that cost over six billion dollars[169] what you are left with is not a representative of the people. In a system so dependent and focused on capital you could be left with a choice between corrupt politicians or highly compromised billionaires.

The forefront messages within political campaigns are rarely our biggest collective challenges. None of the big players truly fight for switching to sustainable energy as soon as possible, nor for feeding and caring for those in need, free health care, free education, removing money from politics, abolishing lobbying and tax havens, making governments and corporations transparent and accountable, moving away from consumer-based economies, and creating self-sufficient empowered communities. These can never be at the forefront of their campaigns as these solutions go against the primary goal of the modern political and corporate system: that is, increased private revenue. More authentic solutions could cut ties with corporate funding leaving them mute in a contest of volume.

Barack Obama was, broadly speaking, viewed as more popular and progressive than Hillary or Trump. However, during National Native American Heritage Month he allowed the oil pipeline construction through the land of the Standing Rock Sioux Tribe[170]. Teargas, rubber bullets and other violent and inhumane methods were used to attack peaceful protesters. Even the widely praised 'liberal' Canadian President Justin Trudeau went against the public's wishes and supported corporate interests when he approved huge oil pipeline expansions during the wake of the U.S. election[171]. Our leaders are supporting billionaires, even when their 'solutions' are temporary, harmful and go against the direct wishes and rights of the people. Even political figures who appear genuine and compassionate are often restricted by a deeply compromised political party.

"Private interests have captured large parts of the government ... it's just

very hard for ordinary people's issues to get attention when there's that much money on the other side."
-Jane Mayer

Our politicians regularly commit a vast percentage of their time in office trying to win the next election by any means possible. This involves ensuring the support of media outlets and the continued financial donations of large corporations. As former Senate Majority Leader Tom Daschle noted, money-gathering efforts can make up around two-thirds of a politician's schedule[172]. So what happens when a country's leader is asked by the public to put pressure on a given corporation, and that corporation decides to donate billions to said leader? At the very least we can say they are highly compromised when they receive private funding. We have systems in place which allow our politicians to listen to corporations over the will of the people and scientific evidence.

The more you dig, the more you will find masses of filthy money behind each of our leaders. Philip May, husband to U.K Prime Minister Theresa May, is a senior executive at a $1.4tn investment fund that profits from tax-avoiding companies[173]. Trump's list of infamous donors includes private prisons, the tobacco industry, and Pfizer[174], the world's most powerful drug company, who are infamous for receiving one of the largest criminal fines in U.S. history–$2.3bn–for "mispromoting medicines and for paying kickbacks to compliant doctors."[175] And Hillary Clinton's election campaign received over $6.9 million from lobbyists, bundlers and large donors connected to the fossil fuel industry[176].

"Politicians should wear sponsor jackets like Nascar drivers, then we would know who owns them."
-Robin Williams

I am not suggesting that people no longer vote nor would I suggest that your vote is futile. Some candidates are better than others and may well provide a great deal of damage limitation. What I am suggesting is that, broadly speaking, our current 'choices', and more importantly, our current political processes, are inherently flawed. And when we place our votes at the ballot box, there is no option for "Neither. Please try again." With the remaining two candidates in the U.S. Election, neither were offering sufficient and authentic systemic change. And perhaps what we've experienced since, at the systemic level, is spectacle on the outside, continuity and solidification on the inside. Regardless of who was the best choice, both candidates were deeply compromised and incredibly self-serving. America needs a leader that is for the people before they are for themselves, large corporations, and even their own political party. The current system does not facilitate this.

## Hypernormalisation

The term hypernormalisation was coined in Alexei Yurchak's book *Everything was forever, until it was no more*[177]. The book explores Soviet life during the period leading up to the collapse of the Soviet Union. The term is used to describe a surreal state of mind where people suspect that things aren't quite right and that the system is failing. Before the collapse of the Soviet Union the people knew they had lost control and were not being told the whole truth. During this unsettling feeling of hypernormalisation, the public carried on as though everything was normal.

In his latest film*, Adam Curtis demonstrates how these same feelings are rising up within modern-day capitalism. He explains how our artificial systems are often guided by corporations and the financial sector, and kept stable by politicians who "allow a great deal of corruption to carry on without doing much about it."[178]

Modern examples of hypernormalisation are particularly potent when a highly conservative politician speaks of real change and calls for equality, sustainability and community within our consumer-focused capitalist model.

---

* *HyperNormalisation* (*BBC*, 2016)

They know they are unauthentic. We know they are unauthentic. And they know that we know. It's like a stage play, a surreal form of dramatic irony, where the audience slowly become aware but those in the play continue to act oblivious. We can begin to live in a spectacle, outside of real notions, integrity, and authentic, collective intent. We start to become subject to a story, one that maintains our status quo and greatly displeases us. Our resentment increases as we see more images that don't make sense. Proven and unchallenged evidence begins to mount that political statements are neither truthful nor accountable. As Adam Curtis notes, "new lies are built on top of old lies."[179]

A danger of hypernormalisation is acceptance, remaining passive and even maintaining or perpetuating the suffering caused by a disingenuous system. Genuine change or progressive alternatives can begin to feel more like empty rhetoric. We often reduce our apparent solutions to statements with no real intent behind them. Or worse still, many will adopt a highly cynical, nihilistic philosophy.

## Follow the Money

Another key point to take away from the work of Adam Curtis and the concept of hypernormalisation is that our current system is more complicated than traditional capitalism or neoliberalism*. Our systems are now an intricate melding of conservative politics, mainstream media perception management, large corporate control, and the financial and banking sectors, thus creating an almost post-democratic, managerial corporate politics. This creates a confusing combination with no identifiable or visible decision makers, except perhaps power itself or those in the quest thereof.

Perhaps the only way to find the source of power is to use the ever-valid cliché: follow the money. Upon doing so we see a surge of new influencers throughout recent times. It was once the tobacco industries who called the

---

* Neoliberalism is often viewed as an aggressive form of capitalism which favours the private sector. It is often criticised for austerity, deregulation, and offshoring wealth.

shots, then we saw the pharmaceutical and sugar corporations, and now we have a rise in tech companies such as Microsoft, Google and Facebook. Each dominant influencer has its own holy cash cow; a money-making commodity in high demand. What is troubling about current times is the resource in demand is data. Therefore those at the top are increasingly equipped to maintain a constant flow of consumption. They can market specifically to individuals through highly adaptive bespoke campaigns. They can learn from our patterns, habits and routines, creating ever-intelligent marketing strategies, appearing as an almost artificial intelligence. It knows when it's your birthday, when you're on holiday, and when you've moved house or got a new job. It knows where you are and what you last searched for or purchased online. It learns what images, texts, fonts and colours are most clickable. It can invent addictions and fixes, problems and solutions; an ever-evolving supply and demand loop which moulds to your current situation and preferences. This is not an 'evil puppet master' but the power of harvesting data, tracking patterns and targeting keywords. It can then execute highly efficient, tried and tested formulae, such as people in category ABC are more likely to be susceptible to marketing tactic XYZ. It will execute the relevant formula, track the results and make amendments to strategies accordingly.

These corporations are not bound by the same restrictions as states. They can rebrand, set up sister companies, buy up competitors and continuously expand their 'borders'. They can be extremely efficient at promoting more consumption. Therefore, our governments are in many ways forced to support them as they 'need' to catch up with a runaway debt crisis. This is particularly troubling when you consider that only 5 countries* in the world are debt free[180]. Therefore nearly all of our politicians will only continue to facilitate and promote further increases of consumption, even though overconsumption is already killing us, our wildlife and bleeding our natural resources dry. This is evident in the harrowing clip when George W. Bush— moments after updating the public on the war in Iraq—encouraged us all to go shopping[181]. The answer appears to always be more consumption. Spend, spend, spend, and let our communities, our health and our planet pay the

* Macao, British Virgin Islands, Brunei, Liechtenstein, and Palau.

price. Going shopping is what we do to 'repair' the economy. It is how we prop up a failing system, but also how we get spikes of dopamine in an unfulfilling environment that lacks genuine human connection. Retail therapy becomes our most prescribed medicine.

# Magic Money Tree

In the UK, every single day, 200 women and children escaping domestic violence cannot find safe refuge as a result of heartless austerity measures[182]. The victims are often in their pyjamas carrying whatever belongings they can manage, as escaping in the middle of the night can be the safest option. However, when they arrive at the doors of a safe house, they are turned away due to a lack of funding.

Sadly this is far from an isolated incident as brutal cuts take place all around the world. In the U.S. for example, 9 million children recently had their health insurance taken away from them as a result of 'necessary' austerity measures[183].

The response from our politicians is the same old line: "There simply isn't enough money to go around." Or worse, the incredibly patronising, "There's no magic money tree." Unfortunately, this is a very attractive soundbite as it implies a common sense and a rejection of irrational witchcraft. And therefore, we accept that there is 'nothing' that can be done: case closed.

However, if we take a look at the U.S. to see if there really is a lack of funds, it poses important questions such as, what about the:

· Recent tax breaks for the top 1%?[184]
· The $4 billion in oil subsidies each year?[185]
· Last years' 12 billion dollar bonus for Wall Street Bankers?[186]
· The $111 billion in revenue lost each year due to offshore accounts?[187]
· The $700 billion bank bailout?[188]
· The current military budget of 825 billion dollars?[189]

And, what about the U.S. President himself, bragging about not paying tax for 18 years?[190]

While standards are declining, profits are rising. And those who need our help the most cannot purchase a voice in our pay-to-play 'democratic' system; therefore they are the worst hit by cuts.


# Privatising in Private


"I'm not looking to overthrow the American government, the corporate state already has."

-John Trudell


With mounting evidence that humans significantly contribute to global warming, it was a great achievement when 195 countries agreed to lowering emissions in 2015[191]. It therefore seemed bewildering to many when President Donald Trump withdrew from the Paris Climate Agreement in 2017. This decision was accompanied by greater confusion when Trump added that the U.S. "will continue to be the cleanest and most environmentally friendly country on Earth."[192]–a very conflicting statement coming from the biggest carbon-polluting country in history[193]. This is a perfect example of 'alternative facts', hypernormalisation, and the infamous doublespeak*. Then again, perhaps his actions shouldn't have been such a shock. Not only is Trump heavily funded by oil and coal corporations, so too were the 22 senators who asked Trump to withdraw from the agreement[194]. Senator Ted Cruz, for example, was reported as receiving over $2.5 million from oil, gas and coal corporations[195]. The Paris Climate Agreement wasn't even binding, and still the U.S. government went back on its word, despite the international backlash and despite the harm that it will cause to us all and the environment.

Another example of going back on one's word can be found in Trump's

---

\* Doublespeak is language that can distort or redefine definitions, sometimes used to create ambiguity, confusion, and hide the truth.

*Meet The Press* interview when he stated, "No matter what you do, guns no guns, it doesn't matter. You have people that are mentally ill and they're going to come through the cracks."[196] The hypocrisy and confusion comes from the fact that he later signed a bill allowing mentally ill people to buy guns. Again, once you scratch beneath the surface, you start to find an explanation–the National Rifle Association donated $30 million to Trump's presidential campaign[197].

"What Donald Trump's cabinet of billionaires and multimillionaires represents is a simple fact: the people who already possess an absolutely obscene share of the planet's wealth ... are determined to grab still more."
-Naomi Klein

The UK National Health Service (NHS) is deeply important to nearly every UK citizen. It is one of the few remaining free public services that commits to protecting lives, 24-hours a day, 7 days a week. However, the NHS is currently collapsing. It is under-supported, pushed to its limits and being sold off piecemeal to private corporations. This quickly becomes explainable as many UK Members of Parliament (MPs) have direct financial links to private health care firms. In 2014, The Mirror released a list of 70 MPs with comprising connections, which included: David Cameron, former Conservative Prime Minister; Andrew Lansley, former Conservative Health Secretary; Greg Barker, former Conservative Energy Minister; and David Davis, former Conservative Shadow Home Secretary[198].

While it may be more exciting to imagine a 'heartless overlord' whispering into the ears of our sidekick politicians, backlit and cackling as people are dying in hospital waiting rooms, what if they are simply advisors? Individuals who unfortunately, in a deeply flawed and immoral system, can be bought? What if this further increases the revenue of private corporations and therefore further increases their power and influence? What if the system has evolved in such a way that politicians have to constantly reduce government spending while promoting further consumption to chase a run-away debt?

We have to acknowledge that private corporations can buy political reform and in many cases can completely overpower the democratic vote. Clearly people don't want irreparable harm for themselves or the planet, but private corporations do want more money and, sadly, in our post-democratic system their money frequently overpowers our legitimate concerns.

When the wealthiest people fund the party they feel will protect their profits, we enter a cyclical process where those with money shape their own systems. Hillary Clinton, not known to shy away from warfare, was heavily funded by the most powerful arms dealers in the world[199]. Donald Trump, infamous for his xenophobia, received an enormous amount of support from white supremacist organisation the Ku Klux Klan[200]. Those who protect immoral acts can in turn receive money which can then be spent on more marketing which can lead to more votes. If we have a party that represents the poorest members of society, they can become overshadowed by expensive marketing campaigns.

Within our post-democratic, corporate managerial politics we can see former symbols of public services such as prisons, hospitals and schools become privatised entities with a direct focus on capital. As Groucho Marx once noted, even a hospital bed has become a parked taxi with the meter running[201]. As our former public services become wealthy businesses, the people start to question, where does our tax money go? In fact, the question of taxation becomes ever more pertinent when we see increasing instances of tax avoidance, not just from large corporations, but politicians and even the queen of England[202]. Are those in charge out to get as much private revenue as possible? Have they become those who privatize in private?

Money has shaped politics. Cruel and unsustainable acts can be justified, if profitable. Billionaire investors buying properties and forcing out locals can be viewed as, at the governmental level, 'good' for the people as it can funnel more money into the economy. This may defy logic, but it is how our current model works. Nearly every country is in debt, therefore money is the target.

Removing restrictions on harmful energy resources can be justified as restrictions can mean competition to profit. Subsidizing unhealthy fast food products can attract large corporations and therefore increase revenue. And allowing increasing amounts of advertising tactics which target our children's vulnerabilities can be incredibly profitable.

Politics was once viewed as being a way to provide a voice to those unheard against the powerful. Now it seems as though our two-party system can become one corporation's vision of the future versus another's. And with the addition of Donald Trump, both metaphorically and now quite literally, highly compromised corporations are running our countries.

# 20/20 Politics

We have to create alternatives, new systems where the Donald Trumps of the world are no longer necessary. I can see no positive change coming from insulting or silencing those who blaspheme against Saint Hillary. I can also see no value in hurling abuse at Trump and his supporters. The more we victimise Trump and those who voted for him, the more we divide, and Hillary and traditional politicians could be viewed as a genuine solution to the world's problems. It is counterproductive and hypocritical to attack the voters of either side, especially during a time when unity is so vital.

The change we need cannot come from the superficial administrative level of modern-day politics; it will come from outside of its corruption. Neither party, in its current form, is a viable solution. We have a duty to create a better world when the system so clearly fails us. We should be wary of divisive arguments and distractions during these times and look towards united and authentic solutions to the root of our collective challenges.

Let Donald Trump be a blessing in disguise as it is no longer possible to ignore the painful joke that has become our current political system. It was exponentially easier to conceal self-serving interests behind slick spokesmen, ones who are well-groomed with decades of training in political diplomacy. Trump is a global ice-breaker. He is the rupture that exposes not just concealed grotesque crimes but the myth of unlimited consumption, the denial of science and limitations, and the abandonment of compassion and community. He is like a broken bone in the old skeleton of capitalism. You cannot ignore a broken bone. It causes too much suffering. When we complete the x-ray, we will discover many more wounds that have been left untreated. It would be a missed opportunity for him to become a scapegoat, one which is falsely diagnosed as the root cause of our current pain. He is merely a symptom, and perhaps a fantastic opportunity to really contemplate not only what is happening in the U.S, but all around the world; not just with regards to capitalism and consumerism, but the very ideas of ownership, harmful narratives, divisive systems, stockpiling wealth, advertising, materialism and isolated power.

If we reduce our current woes to one individual we are forgetting a key fact: reductiveness played a part in creating the very situation that we find ourselves in. We need to collectivize and actively seek and discuss new solutions. There is a huge difference between being a good person and being a proactive good person. If a good person finds themself in a situation, they will try to do the right thing within that limited range, whereas a proactive good person will go out of their way to physically try to make the world a better place. Let's become part of a solution rather than wishfully waiting for a slight improvement. You won't make large companies pay taxes, improve their practices or share their profits by continuing with business as usual. However, you can spark discussions, work together and proactively find and create alternatives.

"Freethinkers are those who are willing to use their minds without prejudice and without fearing to understand things that clash with their own customs, privileges, or beliefs."
-Leo Tolstoy

Many people avoid watching documentaries or reading books about how our food and other products are made as they don't want to feel guilty. They'd rather maintain their current malpractice through denial than try to improve. Others will ignore world news as they are tired of corruption and feeling empathy for those in need. And many of us refuse to explore alternative systems as we believe that we have no real capacity for change. Now, more than ever, we need to unite and become beacons of hope, offering clear solutions and proactively leading by example. We can start with self-reflection, in turn becoming better people who make sustainable, fair and respectful choices that we can be proud of. We can reshape the world we live in by questioning all aspects of our lives because all of our actions have direct consequences: how we get to work, where we work, what we eat and what we buy. If we lift our heads up from the artificial glowing screens of our shiny new smartphones and embrace the challenges that we collectively face, we can make a real difference. If we avoid the transient highs of consumerism and shift to a grounded purpose, we can become more sustainable, healthier and happier. If we remain committed and determined in the face of overwhelming challenges, we can accomplish anything. If we try our hardest we cannot lose. This is the essence of proactive, direct action.

"An idea whose time has come cannot be stopped by any army or any government."
-Ron Paul

Neither Trump nor Hillary are the real problem; attacking them is attacking the symptoms. They are the consequences of corruption and a system that fetishises power and money. They are the inevitable fulfilment of our current dangerous trends. Our systems will continue to produce these kinds of leaders unless we change course.

How fitting would it be if by the year 2020 we collectively began to see clearly with 20/20 vision and catch all the immoral and unsustainable acts that take place every day? Through actively engaging we can see what companies and systems share our values, morals and standards. We can then consciously choose whether to maintain and promote them. By opening ourselves up to criticism we can question the morality and sustainability of our own actions and by working together, sharing resources and creative direct action we can create better systems that serve our collective needs. And if we don't, we'll end up with more disenfranchised and divided people, more inequality, more suffering, more guilt, more fear and more Donald John Trumps.

Before we fully embrace the solutions and strategies, there is one more area that I feel we need to explore: community. Are we drifting apart? Are there modern communities that have implemented new systems?

CHAPTER 6

# TRIBES

Does scale corrupt?

"Capitalism forgets that life is social."

-Martin Luther King Jr.

Although we often live in urban areas with populations in the millions, we may be mentally confined to a smaller community of deeper relationships. Evolutionary psychologist Robin Dunbar suggested we have a biological limit to the number of people who we can know on a personal level. That number is roughly 150, which is referred to as Dunbar's Number. 150 is not the number of our closest relationships nor people we simply recognise, it is the hypothesised, natural community size of meaningful connections.

Dunbar's research began with studying the socially complex societies of primates; which are facilitated by their large brain size. This led to the hypothesis that one could predict the group size of an animal based on the size of their brain. In turn, through calculations based on the size of the human brain, Dunbar arrived at his now famous number, to which he found many correlating case study examples including parishes, historical villages, business organisations and autonomous military units, all of which tended to have an average size of almost exactly 150[203]. Dunbar's number has appeared in studies spanning vast timeframes, from the common size of hunter-gatherer communities to modern day Twitter and email groups[204].

As a group grows larger, individuals are less observed and may consequently feel less accountable for their actions. An example of this is the Bystander Effect. This is where individuals are more likely to walk past an injured person in a busy street, or just stop and stare, rather than getting involved in the situation. However, if there was no one else around to help, most people will step up.

A larger group size can also reduce our sense of democracy. Personal concerns can become diluted as our voices can become lost in the crowd. Despite being surrounded by more people, we can feel less connected.

Through strong localised political systems and technological advancements we could one day surpass biological and physical community restrictions. Within our current systems, however, the consequences of scale cannot be ignored.

## The Room Experiment

To give a more visual example of the challenges of scale, I'd like to pose a series of questions through a hypothetical experiment: The Room Experiment.

Imagine you are a volunteer researcher. You have been asked to be the sole monitor for an experiment which will study how two participants cope in a confined space with an unknown person. They will be placed in a small white room which has neither windows nor furniture. You will be monitoring the experiment through the use of hidden cameras and microphones. As the study conditions are designed to push the participants to their limits, they will only receive one small meal and one glass of water each per day.

As the experiment begins, you feel at ease. Participants in the experiment have chosen a corner each to sit in and are talking to one another amicably.

For note-taking and anonymity purposes, one of them is labeled A and the other is labeled B. You notice that A has sat next to the trap door where, incidentally, the food will arrive. As the day draws to an end they both fall asleep. At 4 a.m. a tray slides into the room accidentally waking up A, who notices the trapdoor. On the tray are two small plates of food and two small glasses of water. A is clearly very hungry and eats all of the contents from one of the plates and drinks a whole glass of water. He waits a moment, looks at the sleeping form of B and makes the decision to eat the food from the second plate. He silently pushes the empty plates and the empty cup through the trapdoor, leaving just a single glass of water remaining. A wipes his mouth, checks there is no remaining evidence, and goes back to sleep.

At 8.a.m B wakes up A and offers to share the remaining cup of water– unaware of what has happened. B mentions that he is starting to feel very unwell due to the lack of food. A doesn't confess to his early-morning actions, and they both share the single glass of water, rationing it throughout the day.

Every night the food arrives at 4.a.m, and every night A eats all of the food and hides the evidence. By day three you notice that B is becoming visibly very ill: shaking, vomiting and crying out in pain. A still doesn't confess, instead pretending to be hungry himself.

Bearing in mind that you can do as you wish, and you are under no obligation to continue the experiment, would you intervene? Would you stop it?

Let's suppose that you allow it to continue. On day 8, B dies. You call an ambulance. The experiment is over, and A goes home. Would you report the truth?

These may seem like obvious questions–more than likely, as you read though the situation, you are firm in the knowledge that you would of course stop the experiment. You wouldn't stand there and do nothing, watching someone steal while someone else is in clear distress and pain. And you would certainly intervene well before B died.

With that as a base level, let's introduce the consequences of scale. Would you act the same way if there were five people in the room, and four of them stole the food while the fifth person starved? Would you intervene if there were 100 people, and 90 people ate while 10 people starved? What if there were 900 people and 100 people didn't have enough food? Would you see it as someone else's job to intervene?

In theory, you may argue that scale would in no way affect your moral judgment. Yet this is the very situation we find ourselves in today. The world's wealthiest eight people own nearly the same as half of the world's population combined[205]. We know that others will go without these riches–or even the bare necessities–through no fault of their own, just like B. Just as in the Room Experiment, those eight people may have had the fortune to be placed near the food supply, and they might take what they want and let the Bs of the world die.

Of course there are other factors at play in the real-world scenario: factors such as corporations, governments, borders and the media. But if we strip it back to people and resources, then the experiment is not so different.

Is scale, therefore, one of the contributing factors to why we turn a blind-eye to immoral behaviour?

## Is Inequality Healthy?

A study by Doctors Sarah Brosnan and Frans de Waal in which capuchin monkeys were unfairly 'paid' demonstrates the natural and instinctive rejection of inequality[206]. In their study, they give a monkey a small rock. If the monkey returns the rock, they receive food as a reward. The monkeys soon adapt to this concept, quickly returning the rock and expecting 'payment' for their 'labour'. When two caged monkeys were placed side-by-side, Brosnan and de Waal found that the monkeys were happy to complete the task around 25 times in a row, with a cucumber reward for every completed task.

They then introduced the monkeys to the concept of inequality. Instead of 'paying' all of the monkeys with cucumbers, they paid some of them with grapes–considered by the monkeys to be far superior. The test goes as follows:

Monkey A is given a rock which it returns. It is then 'paid' with cucumber, which it eats. Next, monkey B is given a rock which it returns. It is 'paid' with a grape, which it eats. Monkey A, although in a separate cage, was closely watching Monkey B, therefore witnessing the inequality. Monkey A is then given another rock. It returns the rock and is again rewarded with cucumber. This time it throws the cucumber at the scientist and starts hitting the sides of the cage. It becomes visibly very angry at the injustice and tries to escape. It has a zero tolerance to inequality. It instinctively rejects it and rebels.

The difference between a piece of cucumber and a grape may seem minimal, but it represents the notion of an individual being worth more than another. Among social species this can be incredibly disconcerting as it can challenge their very essence.

The scale of inequality in the human species can be enormous, even between those working in the same building, as CEOs have been reported to earn an average of 774 times as much as minimum wage[207]. In fact, global inequality has reached 100-year highs, with the richest 500 people seeing a wealth increase of $1tn last year[208]. Perhaps then, it is no wonder that many are very angry.


## Modern Tribes

"Money brings down the dams of community."
-Yuval Noah Harari


We have seen that money, consumerism, advertising and many other aspects within our current system can harm our communities. We have also seen that scale can corrupt and that even low levels of inequality can be highly traumatic. But are there any communities trying something different?

Auroville, Tamil Nadu, India

On the east coast of southern India is a community of 2,400 people who have their own form of currency. Auroville aims to be a universal town where people can live in peace. The residents believe that the town belongs to no one person but to the greater community. The current residents come from some 49 nations, from all age groups and backgrounds. The people of Auroville are united by a common belief that we can all be born with equal opportunities.

Kailash Ecovillage, Oregon, U.S.A.

While people may assume that sustainable community projects are always 'in the middle of nowhere', here's an example of an ecovillage* apartment block in inner south-east Portland, only four miles from downtown. The site is complete with rainwater catchments, solar power, living roofs, shared kitchens, passive heating techniques, communal areas, vehicle shares, permaculture gardens and micro-forestry projects. With an incredibly strong collaborative community it's no wonder that it has a growing waiting list: a clear sign many of us are looking for more sustainable, ethical and social ways of living. The community has the following mission statement: "Kailash Ecovillage is a community committed to providing a sustainable, beautiful and safe living environment for individual residents as well as the greater community."[209]

Steward Woodland Community, Devon, England

In Dartmoor National Park in south-west England lies a self-sufficient, off-the-grid community. In exchange for the land, they help to maintain the surrounding area. When an issue arises in the group, meetings are called and the residents take it in turn to air their concerns. This prevents resentments and frustrations by ensuring that everybody is heard. One member mentions a

---

* Communities are often referred to as an Ecovillage if they dramatically reduce their environmental impact. Those within the communities are often practicing sustainable ways of living as well as seeking a greater sense of community.

lot of people in today's society are "very depressed, unhappy and feel unfulfilled."[210] He admits that he himself was depressed and had problems with drugs. However, he reveals since he has connected with nature and surrounded himself with a supportive community, his life has changed for the better. The people of the community have become empowered through self-sufficiency to live free, healthy, communicative and fulfilling lives.

## Konohana Family, Honshu Island, Japan

At the foot of Mount Fuji is a tightly-knit, agricultural community. The community has a collective economy through sharing meals, resources and finances. They cultivate over 250 types of vegetables and grains as well as raising chickens for eggs and bees for honey. As they are largely self-sufficient, they greatly reduce their environmental impact.

To give a simplified sustainability value to certain ways of life, they can be given a score with 1 representing 100% of the planet's bio-capacity. Therefore if everybody on the planet had a score of 2, we would need two planet Earths to continue that way of life. The Konohana Family are running at a reported 0.8, making them a sustainably viable community[211].

## The Farm, Tennessee, U.S.A

Located in Lewis County, Tennessee, is one of America's first post-industrialisation intentional communities. A large group of people seeking a community-focused, sustainable, non-violent and environmentally sound way of life combined all of their funds to purchase 1,750 acres of land. The community now has an impressive decentralized infrastructure including their own electrical crews, agricultural departments, schools, bakery, energy grid, construction team, ambulance service, book publishing company and tofu plant. They have also started their own charitable projects to help those outside of the community, including natural disaster aid relief.

## Free and Real, Mount Telaithrion, Greece

On the slopes of Mount Telaithrion is a self-sufficient, rural community created by 4 young Greeks who became dissatisfied by consumer culture and wanted to escape the rat race. The group has grown over time with many of their current members giving up high-paying jobs to explore and promote a free way of life. One member noted that people watching TV and reading the news will be bombarded with crisis after crisis and yet "here there is no crisis."[212]

The community helps and inspires others through social media, seminars and its own self-sufficiency school. One of the founding members explains, "I just tried to be the change that I want to see, instead of waiting for governments to make the change."[213] The people of the community are united by a passion to lead by example as well as proactively helping and supporting others to do the same.

## Mangrove Mountain Yoga Ashran, Mangrove Creek, Australia

A one-hour drive from Sydney lies a yogic agricultural community. Volunteers, students, and residents can live for free, as they share shelter, food, water and other resources in exchange for community contributions. The work schedule is roster-based where tasks such as maintenance, farming and cooking are shared equally among the group. This fosters a non-competitive, encouraging and supportive environment.

## Copeaux Cabana, Dordogne, France

In the south of France, a group of carpenters and friends began building tiny homes in the woods. They live off the grid and share free labour amongst each other. They say that working as a collective and collaborating on projects can provide numerous mental health benefits.

Alongside traditional practices they invent their own sustainable techniques such as a bicycle-powered wood lathe. They also work with their environment, using mud for insulation and the natural curves in the trees to form the shapes of their homes. The community is united by a love of working with nature amongst friends.

Kovcheg Village, Kaluga, Russia

In 2001, four families leased nearly 300 acres of land south-west of Moscow. This eventually became a sustainable village of around 120 people. The community share an eco-friendly lifestyle and work together to protect and maintain the surrounding area. Many of the residents left 'successful' jobs in search of a more justifiable, rewarding and sustainable way of life. Residents include former wrestlers, models, singers and even a politician. The founder was once a businessman but is now a beekeeper, gardener and happy contributor to his community.

Earthaven, Black Mountain, North Carolina

On 329 acres of land in North Carolina lies an off-the-grid, sustainable ecovillage. Some of their goals include: to shift from wasteful to regenerative use of resources; to catalyse local and global change through learning, teaching, and networking; and to practice healthy, holistic lifestyles that balance self-care with care for others. The community share renewable energy sources and have created various edible landscapes to provide ample free food. Although the people of Earthaven frequently collaborate, it is broken in to a series of smaller neighbourhoods allowing members to practice their own ways of life. All members undergo consensus decision training as they are invited to help collectively guide the development of the site.

La ZAD, Notre-Dame-des-Landes, France

In 2009 a large scale, anti-capitalist land occupation took place in north-west France and is continuing today. The protest was in response to the announcement that a new airport would be built in a highly biodiverse agricultural area. There is already an airport nearby and the public wanted to protect the land and its residents rather than pursue additional corporate economic gains. The peaceful protesters quickly built a small settlement on the site to defend the area from urbanisation. Armed forces have frequently attacked the residents with rubber bullets, tear gas and the destruction of various settlements; however, the occupiers are still there, and remain positive, passionate, peaceful and united. Thousands from around the world, of all ages and backgrounds, have united to help the community through supplies, labour and support. The occupiers are building more settlements and increasing agricultural yields to produce abundance for the community. They share free produce, free labour and collectively decide on new actions. The people of ZAD* stand strong in the face of capitalism and are living examples of proactive, non-violent action.

### Dancing Rabbit, Missouri, U.S.A

In north-east Missouri is an ecovillage and sustainability demonstration project. Although the residents have full autonomy and are free to lead independent lives, they frequently collaborate and share resources such as kitchens, electric vehicles, tools, agricultural plots, communal spaces and a free sustainable energy grid. The residents aim to be as sustainable as possible and follow strict eco-building guidelines. As a result they have been able to reduce their consumption of water, electricity, natural gas and vehicle miles by 90% below that of the average American household. Like many of the other eco-communities the residents actively inspire others and openly share resources and knowledge, allowing others to learn from their mistakes and successes.

### Findhorn Ecovillage, Moray, Scotland

In north-east Scotland lies an experimental ecovillage founded in the 1980s. Their buildings are made from found materials, four wind turbines supply their free energy grid, they share zero-emission vehicles, and their water treatment plant makes use of algae, snails and various plant life to filter and purify the water supply–which they aptly named a living machine. In a recent study, researchers concluded that the residents have the lowest ecological footprint of any community measured in the industrialised world[214].

### Global Community Movement

Many more communities around the world are creating their own solutions

---

* The term ZAD means Zone to Defend (French: zone à défendre)

with many of them being part of the following groups: the intentional communities movement, the ecovillage movement, and the permaculture movement.

From the examples we have seen, it is clear that people can regain control of their lives, practicing their own beliefs and living in strong, compassionate communities. These communities could have been viewed as naïve utopian dreams, but now they are reality and proof that you don't always have to follow a system that doesn't serve you or your planet.

In most cases these communities are also helping the rest of us by drastically decreasing their environmental impact, and maintaining, creating, and promoting sustainable techniques. They act as a reminder that self-sufficiency is not a step back into the Dark Ages nor a life of isolation. These people are living abundant lives and remain connected to the rest of the world. They also frequently report their new-found happiness and sense of pride in their new way of life, without a focus on money or material consumption.

While the groups mentioned above have been able to peel away from the current system through small-scale complementary projects, what about larger systemic change? This is what we'll explore in the next chapter through a whole new political system that aims to tackle many of the concerns raised thus far.

Our current systems are hundreds of years old, based on tools and practices that are thousands of years old; now is the time to explore something better.

"You cannot solve a problem from the same consciousness that created it; you must learn to see the world anew."
-Albert Einstein

# PART II

# HOW CAN WE HELP?

The Big Picture: A whole new system

# CHAPTER 7
# FOUNDATIONS

What's the alternative?

U p to this point we have attempted to decipher and decode our current system. We dug deep to explore some common pain points and root causes. Now it is time to explore a brighter future; for if we can't even imagine a better scenario, how will we achieve it?

"The interplay between lofty dreams and earthly victories has always been at the heart of moments of deep transformation. The breakthroughs won for the workers and their families after the Civil War and during the Great Depression, as well as for civil rights and the environment in the sixties and early seventies, were not just responses to crises. They were responses to crises that unfolded in times when people dared to dream big."
-Naomi Klein

This is a chance to think about the bigger picture and start from scratch. We don't have to inherit ancient tools and dated concepts in our own imagination. We can explore new possibilities through a hypothetical system— The Free System. Even if it is unrealistic or 'too forward thinking', it can be a useful practice to explore an ideal scenario. We can think about the potential challenges and opportunities of a new system as well as how we could improve or implement it. We can also think about how it differs from the systems that we have in place today. It can offer us new perspectives as well as a potential destination.

"A map of the world that does not include Utopia is not worth even glancing at, for it leaves out the one country at which Humanity is always landing. And when Humanity lands there, it looks out, and, seeing a better country, sets sail. Progress is the realization of Utopia."
-Oscar Wilde

In the final section of this book, we move away from hypothetical solutions and explore real-world action items that we can implement today. For now, though, let's dare to think big and explore what a whole new system could look like.

## The Free System

"You never change things by fighting the existing reality. To change something, build a new model that makes the existing model obsolete."
-Richard Buckminster Fuller

In the quest for clarity, let's begin with the name. The word 'free' refers to the system's intentions: to facilitate a world free from slavery, dictatorships and dated tools and traditions that are holding us back from reaching our true potential. A world free from unsustainable and unethical practices. A world free from money, a focus on money or money as the primary goal. A world liberated from divisive structures founded on ego and ownership.

Free also refers to the fact that the system is 'anonymous'. It is not tied to a person, corporation or political party. The problems don't belong to any one person and neither should the solutions. We should remove any barriers that prevent us becoming engaged. The Free System is not so much a ready-made complete solution, rather a free set of ideas that I encourage others to draw from. It is not an all-or-nothing fixed system and it is free to evolve. The ideas are modular to facilitate this.

The Free System is completely different to those offered by mainstream political parties. It is not capitalism, socialism or communism. It is not left-wing or right-wing–it is a different bird. It is a new chance to unite. Let's explore version 1.0.

## United Goals

The capitalist system can no longer be viewed as a soaring success, and yet it seems that the left-wing and right-wing are fighting, only accelerating their collective downfall. To reach new heights we need unity. We need to collaborate and prioritise. And we can start by deciding the minimum system requirements that we can all agree on.

Along with future generations, we all need the same things to survive: clean air, clean water, nutritious food and adequate shelter. We have far more in common than the things that seemingly separate us. We all want peace and security. Everyone wants to live happy, healthy and fulfilling lives. Our systems should at the very least prioritise survival, sustainability and general well-being.

To ensure that we remove distractions and focus on what really matters, our hypothetical system will be accountable to clear targets. These goals will be fair, rational and unifying.

The six united goals of the Free System are as follows: Community, Happiness, Equality, Ethics, Freedom and Sustainability (C.H.E.E.F.S):

Sustainability: because it's not right, responsible or practical to consume, produce or support something at the expense of someone else, present or future. Sustainability is a crucial goal that has been largely ignored in our current systems. Sustainability is not limited to renewable energy sources and environmental protection. It also includes the sustainability of our own good health, both physical and mental. The want of money should never supersede our need for sustainability.

Equality: because it's not right for some to be free whilst others are enslaved. It's not right that some bathe in lavish abundant lifestyles whilst others go without basic human needs. It's not fair that some receive free education and free health care, whilst others are denied. It is morally indefensible that nationality, race, gender, inheritance, sexual orientation or any other non-chosen trait can greatly impact one's human rights. Life doesn't have to be a cruel and unjust lottery. We could empower everyone with the same rights that we would like to be awarded.

Ethics: because there's an ethical alternative for everything that we need. We could become a role model society who can stand by our actions. We can demand full transparency from corporations and ethical practices that are in line with our own values. We shouldn't have to repress guilt or shame; we could be proud of our systems.

Freedom: because land, water and natural resources should not be owned by private corporations. We do not have to live a life focused on continuously consuming and acquiring money and material possessions. We don't have to accept systems that encroach on our personal freedom.

Community: because we can transition away from systems of competition and greed, towards those of collaboration, connection, and contribution. We don't have to use systems that facilitate or reward irresponsible and harmful acts. Together we are healthier and stronger.

Happiness: because we would all like to live happy lives, and with new systems focused on sustainability, equality, ethics, freedom and community, we can. We can start living lives that we are truly inspired by, with an authentic, grounded and healthy purpose. We can implement systems that are no longer harmful to others.

The solutions can take many forms and come from all over the world as we collaborate to achieve our united goals. If we agree on rational targets, regardless of political or religious preferences, then we have a great chance at building new systems that work for everyone. These can be seen as common codes of conduct, founding goals that help to create a communal alignment. We can listen to one another and engage in intelligent, respectful debate if we are clear about our intentions.

Without solid goals, past movements have become compromised or even become part of the problem they were once seeking to solve. This effect can be seen when movements towards equality turn into acts of hate and supremacy. Groups can lose sight of goals when a movement shifts towards anger and frustration. By contrast, the goals within our hypothetical system are now clear, defined and open to all. The people can let us know if we are contradicting or undermining our mission. Focusing on what really matters, through clear goals and not fighting over differences, is crucial for our survival.

Please remember this is a hypothetical set of ideas: a chance for us to think big, to start a system from the ground up, without being restricted by current frameworks and ideologies. With that in mind, let's take a look at how some of our collective goals could protect us against our current challenges.

## Safety Nets

Politics can be incredibly unapproachable and confusing. Many of us didn't study it during primary or secondary education. And even those who chose to explore this field as an adult could be excused for not fully understanding the basic input and output functions of the political system.

This situation is made even more confusing as politicians are regularly non-specific in their explanations and unaccountable for their actions. During inter-political debates they heckle one another, frequently talk over the other person and, in many cases, hurl personal abuse. When replying to direct questions they often seem to speak in riddles, repeat unrelated stock lines or flat-out refuse to answer. An example would be Canadian Prime Minister Justin Trudeau who recently avoided answering the exact same direct question* eighteen times in a row within the Canadian House of Commons[215].

The political process can end up appearing as a disingenuous charade which shows a total lack of respect to a service that millions have sacrificed their lives to protect. Accordingly, "Politics is corrupt." becomes an unchallenged soundbite and few are keen to understand or become engaged with the political process.

When creating completely new systems, we can wipe the slate clean and provide a new direction with full clarity. We can simplify the process, remove alienating language and explain the genuine intention behind each layer of governance.

Starting from the ground up requires solid foundations. How can we stop it falling down or not fulfilling its purpose? Of our six collective goals (C.H.E.E.F.S), sustainability and equality will form our first line of defence. They can act as giant safety nets, protecting our new system. These areas can be scientifically measured as we seek to remove ego, power, and 'alternative facts' from decisions that affect us all. Let's take a look at some examples to explore how the safety nets of sustainability and equality could serve the people during times of rapid 'progression'.

Crude Oil

There are two forms of energy: renewable and non-renewable. Oil is a finite, non-renewable resource. Why then, would we build systems based on the power of oil? Why would we continue to invest time, energy and lives into this temporary resource?

---

* The question being, how many times have you met with the ethics commissioner?

Not only is oil physically unsustainable due to its finite nature, but it is also harmful to us, our wildlife, and to clean forms of energy. Why would we build infrastructure based around something that we know pollutes our air, water and food supply?

Oil owners are people who own something that has been there for over 100 million years and is naturally produced by the earth. They are some of wealthiest and therefore some of the most powerful people in the world. They have captured vast areas of land so that they can control a non-renewable and harmful resource. They have then ensured, through various means, that we develop, build and maintain infrastructures based upon this resource. And they will continue to do so, as they are still financially rewarded for these actions.

As Canadian Prime Minister Justin Trudeau recently stated, "No country would find 173 billion barrels of oil in the ground and just leave them."[216] Or put another way, it is difficult to turn one's back on a massive money-making opportunity, even if it does pollute the planet and its inhabitants.

Let's pretend oil was discovered in our new system. As oil is a natural resource we must analyse its compatibility through the founding safety nets. We discover oil and we ask: is it sustainable? Through scientific, peer-reviewed research we discover that it isn't (as it's being used today). We then continue the search for a sustainable and healthy solution, of which, thankfully, there are plenty. In fact, sustainable and clean energy sources have been discovered and rediscovered again and again throughout our history. We have the alternatives right now and they have been proven on a global scale.

Why are we still using oil? Who should be making the decisions as to whether we should continue using it or not? The people? Our leading scientists? Or the oil 'owners'–the ones who make money from its continued use? Moving away from oil is inevitable, as it is finite. However, it is still being used as the primary energy source; it is still unnecessarily causing harm.

Lobbying

In our hypothetical system, financial lobbying would not pass through the equality safety net as the wills and wants of a corporation or wealthy individual could never overpower the will of the people via a democratic vote. In short, the Equality Department would ask: does it benefit the whole or just a select few? Is it fair and just? Does it undermine democracy? Through these rational questions we can see that lobbying does not pass the test and is therefore not eligible for our system.

When reviewing American 'democracy' and the use of lobbying, Princeton University concluded, "The preferences of the average American appear to have only a, minuscule, near zero, statistically non-significant impact upon public policy."[217]

In the future, we will look back at our current systems with great shame as on a daily basis we are ignoring harrowing inequality and carrying out highly unethical and unsustainable practices. Through a new logical system, we could be the change. A new system could ensure that current and future practices are strictly evaluated with regards to sustainability and equality. These safety nets can be applied through scientific assessment with the people's best interests in mind, hence The Free System's motto, "with compassion and science." If, with no amount of money or power, could you circumvent the two founding pillars of sustainability and equality, countless atrocities, past and present, would have never happened. We don't have to witness the results of our current unsustainable and biased systems come to fruition. We can set new standards.

## Distributing Resources

"The waste of plenty is the resource of scarcity."
-Thomas L. Peacock

The United Nations revealed that resolving the world hunger crisis could cost

104

$30 billion a year[218]. To most of us $30 billion is an unimaginable amount of money and therefore it's no surprise that nobody has even dared to tackle this task. However, when looked at with perspective, $30 billion isn't as impossible as it may seem.

In 2012, the U.S. defence budget was over $700 billion[219]. As mentioned previously, America spends more on warfare–incorrectly labeled 'defence'– than any other country in the world[220]. In fact, they spend more than the next eight highest spending countries combined[221]. In 2015, if the U.S. matched the second highest country's 'defence' budget, China–who spent $145 billion[222]– they would still have enough money remaining to solve world hunger 10 times over. You could also argue that making sure that everyone is fed is a far more effective form of defence.

"Why are millions of people still living in poverty when we are more than rich enough to put an end to it once and for all?"
-Rutger Bregman

None of this is an individual attack on the U.S. It is simply an outline of how the funds, resources and solutions that we need for a better world are available today; but our consumer-based system is focused elsewhere. This is not limited to the budget of a nation and how it chooses to distribute its wealth. In fact there are many individuals who could donate $30 billion from their own pockets and still remain within the top 20 wealthiest people on the planet.

According to a 2018 Bloomberg report, the top five richest people in the world are as follows[223]:

| | |
|---|---|
| 1. Jeff Bezos | $114 billion |
| 2. Bill Gates | $94 billion |
| 3. Warren Buffett | $92 billion |
| 4. Mark Zuckerberg | $78 billion |
| 5. Amancio Ortega | $77 billion |

We are living in an age where corporations and even individuals have god-like powers. They can literally choose whether everybody in the world eats or millions continue to die. If feeding the world works out to be a fraction of their wealth, what other gifts could these capitalist 'gods' bestow? Free land, energy, water, travel, health care, education?

If we look at the U.S. discretionary spending of 2015, we can see that over half of the budget is dedicated to Military[224]. We can also see that among the lowest funded departments are Energy, Agriculture, Community Housing, Science, and Environment. What if the public could direct the spending priorities of governments and corporations? What if there was a voting system where you could prioritise resources? What if, at the very least, we could monitor the consequences of our systems?

If we are to create highly optimized systems, we will have to develop new instruments to measure our progress. We currently use tools such as GNP (Gross National Product) or GDP (Gross Domestic Product) to measure our nation's 'success'; however, these can be increased by things such as natural disasters, cancers, wars and political scandals, as these often require huge amounts of spending and new infrastructure.

"Mental illness, obesity, pollution, crime–in terms of the GDP, the more the better. That's also why the country with the planet's highest per capita GDP, the United States, also leads in social problems."
-Rutger Bregman

In our hypothetical system, we can create new tools that are better calibrated to serve and protect the people.

## Earth Stats

The Free System could produce a report card, solutions and suggestions. The government could freely and publicly display vital Earth statistics, including what resources we have left, what we are using and the rate of our consumption. It will warn us when and how resources will be depleted which in turn empowers us to make ethical and sustainable choices.

"Anyone who believes in indefinite growth on a physically finite planet is either mad or an economist."
-Kenneth Boulding


In 2015, the BBC revealed that if everyone on the planet consumed as much as the average American, then we would need five planet Earths[225]. We only have one planet; therefore real drastic change is inevitable*.

Our consumption and resource data is often safe-guarded by governments and corporations, or simply not sought after as the short-sighted goal of money can act as a blinder, keeping us focused on the capitalist rat race. In this dash to individual financial wealth, we regularly compete against other nations, and even our own neighbours. Perhaps in previous times, worldwide statistic updates could have been viewed as a utopian sci-fi concept, yet now it is possible and even partly practiced. We have satellites, advanced scientific tools and instant global communication. We could be clear and transparent and display what we are consuming and the resulting impact. It could include a detailed inventory of resources and the workforce, as well as the number of hours we collectively contributed to make our items. We could have greater control of our lives. We could choose to work more and produce more, if sustainably viable, or work less, consume less, and spend more time with our friends and families, socialising and developing.


## Earth Score and Fair Trade


In addition to a holistic overview via Earth Stats, we could also suggest that

---

* If you'd like to calculate your own planetary consumption value, you can visit footprintcalculator.org

companies can further increase clarity through more responsible product labelling. Perhaps products could display their sustainability value, much like the way we have recommended daily nutritional allowances. These would show how many earths we would need to continue to consume a product based on the frequency of its consumption. In conjunction with Fair Trade certification, this could be a great stride towards equality and sustainability.

We currently see how certain products affect us with regards to their ingredients, but what about how the creation, transportation and consumption of a product impacts others and the environment? Earth Score and Fair Trade seek to turn 'utopian' ideas into real reform. Our supposed right to consume should never be allowed to encroach on the vital human rights of others. Companies may well refuse to display an Earth Score or Fair Trade certification, but the consumers could refuse to purchase a product without one.

In 2017, it was inspiring to see more than 600 global protest marches in support of science[226]. However, it was also very sad to see visible evidence that our governments, media organizations, and corporations choose to ignore and even go against scientific evidence in the pursuit of short-sighted goals.

"By denying scientific principles, one may maintain any paradox."
-Galileo Galilei

As Tony Robbins once said, "it's best to kill the monster while it's a baby, don't wait for it to grow into Godzilla."[227] This is the essence of this movement, not hiding from the truth, proactively doing the best we can and not giving up. Our rational words will be backed by science, and our actions will be the solutions that set us free. We can move away from the 'alternative facts' of ego and profit-driven thinking to solutions backed by grounded truths.

# The Fear of Controversy

"Controversy is only dreaded by the advocates of error."
-Benjamin Rush

Imagine how frustrated we would be if NASA informed us that a meteorite was about to destroy an entire country, and we discover that they have known this information for decades. Worse, if they even had solutions. There is clearly a huge danger in avoiding controversy.

Let's take a look at some modern examples where major issues have been ignored at the risk of our health and futures.

Global Warming

Global warming is a crucial issue because it impacts the lives of everybody on this planet, present and future. The fact that it hasn't been at the forefront of politics is a huge warning sign.

Global warming researchers tell us that:

· Between 2030 and 2050, climate change is expected to cause 250,000 additional deaths per year, from malnutrition, malaria, diarrhoea, and heat stress.[228]
· 15 of the 17 warmest years on record have occurred since 2001.[229]
· Global flooding could triple by 2030.[230]
· Sea levels are rising at their fastest rate in 2,000 years.[231]
· Almost half of plant and animal species have experienced local extinctions due to climate change.[232]
· We now have more greenhouse gases in our atmosphere than any time in human history.[233]

On The Hugh Hewitt Show, Donald Trump stated, "I'm not a believer in global warming."[234] This is a grossly irresponsible statement, especially when you consider that the 2016 paper, *Consensus on Consensus,* revealed that 97% of scientists who have written in peer-reviewed journals say that climate change is real and that it is significantly caused by human activity[235].

You might think that if the climate crisis is that bad, then why aren't thousands of scientists warning us? In fact, they are, and they have been for some time. Most recently over 15,000 scientists from all around the world issued a global warning that we need extreme change in order to save life on Earth[236]. Their concerns included a decline in freshwater availability, forest losses, ocean dead zones, global warming and our unsustainable food practices.

"Refusing to deal with numbers rarely serves the interests of the least well-off."
-Thomas Piketty

Food

Is the food we are eating sustainable? Scientists have recently unveiled some shocking statistics within the world of agriculture. While their findings clearly impact us all, they have not been brought forward by our current governments.

· Animal agriculture is responsible for up to 91% of Amazon destruction.[237]
· 1/3 of the planet is desertified, with livestock as the leading driver.[238]
· A farm with 2,500 dairy cows produces the same amount of waste as a city of 411,000 people.[239]
· A meat eater's diet requires 18 times more land than a plant-based diet.[240]
· The livestock business generates more greenhouse gas emissions than all forms of transport combined.[241]
· Emissions for agriculture are projected to increase 80% by 2050.[242]
· Animal agriculture is the leading cause of species extinction[243], ocean dead zones[244], habitat destruction[245], water pollution[246] and global warming[247].

As animal agriculture has such a significant impact on climate change, it's no surprise the UN has recommended a global move to a meat and dairy-free diet[248]. However, politicians are reluctant to act on the issue. Perhaps because this would create a loss in a given sector, and in this case, a very profitable industry that has a lot of land, wealth and influence.

With over 7.5 billion people to feed, you may think we have to cut corners and maintain compromised food practices. In reality, even our current inefficient systems are producing enough food to feed 10 billion people[249]. In fact, there are more people suffering from obesity worldwide than from hunger[250]. In addition to this, there are a number of ways to not only increase resource efficiency but also sustainability. Therefore the destruction, suffering and the hunger of so many is a choice, a choice made and maintained by those seeking profit and those in control of our policies, ignoring the numbers. These decisions are far too important to be decided behind closed doors, especially by those who may personally benefit from things staying the same.

The crimes around modern food practices reveal the ugliest sides of our system, where those with too much isolated power prioritise money over humanity. Large corporations purchase huge swaths of land in third world countries to grow animal feed. They then transport this to feed the artificially inseminated livestock in another country. Nothing about the industrial livestock process is natural. Each step is determined by what is most cost efficient. Land is taken from those in need to feed profits, not people. 82% of starving children live in countries where food is fed to animals which are eaten by Westerners[251].

We have more efficient, healthy alternatives. Ones which use 18 times less land, less infrastructure and less transportation[252]. Ones which don't require the exploitation of humans, animals nor our natural resources.

Another symptom of our modern food practices is the destruction of biodiversity. Biodiversity is natural and essential for life. When nature is left to its own devices, biodiversity thrives. In remote parts of Borneo, scientists have found more than 700 different species of tree within just 25 acres of land[253]. However, we are now destroying diversity and creating monocultures*, resulting in increased use of water, pesticides and fossil fuels, and a rapid decrease in microorganisms and soil health[254]. We are currently killing off animal and plant species we know nothing about. We are transforming our planet into a factory of a few, profitable and owned products.

Scientists have discovered over 28,000 plants with medicinal properties[255], and we are continuing to discover more. Despite this, up to 137 plant, animal and insect species are lost every day due to rainforest destruction, largely caused by our inefficient food practices[256]. We may be destroying things today that could help us in the future. What if there is an even greater change in climate or new pests threaten some of our current crops? What happens if we have destroyed alternatives? What happens when illnesses develop but we have already killed the cure?

Clothing

Fast Fashion is another part of our lives that we don't question as we are not being made aware of the facts. Companies convince us to buy clothes we don't need to further increase revenue. Here is a breakdown of some key facts highlighted in a recent report:[257]

· The world consumes 80 billion pieces of new clothing each year.

· Many factory workers are not paid a living wage and work in dangerous conditions.

· The fashion industry frequently uses child labour.

· The clothing industry is the second largest polluter of clean water.

· The global cotton industry uses more pesticides than any other crop in the world.

· Over 70 million trees are logged every year for clothing.

· The average American is now generating 82 pounds of textile waste every year.

---

* Monoculture is the practice of growing a single crop over a large area of land.

Again, we can see proof that the right to consume and the right to make profit can have serious consequences. It is hugely irresponsible of our governments to turn a blind eye to these issues as they greatly impact our environments and our health.

Population vs Resources

Another elephant in the room–which governments continue to ignore–is our ever-increasing population, which has skyrocketed at unprecedented rates in recent years. In 1804 we had a population of around one billion, in 1927 we reached two billion; however in 2011, we saw a huge leap to seven billion people[258]. An increase of one billion would have previously taken over a century; now, around a decade[259]. Earth is a finite space with finite resources and yet we are constantly expanding and consuming as though there are no limits–a clear sign that our current political systems are failing.

"If business as usual is allowed to continue, ever-larger expanses of our planet will cease to be hospitable to human life."
-Naomi Klein

In a new system we could be confronted with issues as soon as they appear, giving us more options. Through complete transparency and a responsible attitude to challenging subjects, the people can make better decisions. While the above statistics may be hard-hitting, all of them have proven solutions. New sustainable infrastructures and healthy diets that dramatically reduce our environmental impact exist. Alternative clothing practices are possible and proven*. Reducing, reusing and recycling has a massive impact. And we have seen mounting evidence that when countries are provided with safe food, clean water, reliable infrastructure and education, then the birth rates naturally shift to more sustainable levels[260]. In fact, once communities have solid health and available education systems, employment increases and crime rates fall, among many other benefits.

The impact of animal agriculture, and in particular the beef industry, is so

---

* For more information on sustainable clothing you can visit fashionheroes.eco

profound that if you simply reduce your intake or found a replacement for beef alone–ignoring all other animal products–then you could make a significant improvement to our current climate. Leading scientists from Loma Linda University, Bard College and Oregon State University calculated that if Americans switched from eating beef to beans then the U.S. could still come close to meeting its 2020 greenhouse emission goals, despite withdrawing from the Paris Agreement[261]. This doesn't even include the changes that could be made within the energy and transportation sectors. As noted by environmental researcher Helen Harwatt, "The real beauty of this kind of thing is that climate impact doesn't have to be policy-driven."[262] This is an empowering time as we can personally make a huge difference providing we seek the truth and become engaged.

If someone were to park in the middle of two parking spaces, some people may become aggravated as they are not only unnecessarily using space, they are also selfishly limiting options for others. However, if someone consumes a specific diet or wears certain clothing that uses 20 times the amount of land than someone who uses an alternative, shouldn't we expect people to be at least equally upset? An inefficiently occupied car space may misuse a few meters of concrete, but what about the 80,000 acres of rainforest that we lose every day from avoidable, unsustainable practices?[263] The problem is not 'evil consumers' nor a lack of empathy. The problem lies with a disconnect, a simple lack of awareness–obstacles that challenge profit are kept out of sight.

"We are already using two to three times more of the earth's natural resources than what is sustainable. If we do not act now, we will see the consequences of our depletion of natural resources–and it's not going to be pretty. A desolate, dry Earth is not a fun place to live."
-The World Counts

If we care about the environment and our future we cannot afford to limit our concerns to local issues. What will happen when someone else's water source is depleted or infected? If there isn't enough food will others peacefully die hungry? When people suffer out of sight, the problem doesn't simply disappear, it grows.

With a genuine care of the people, a new system could constantly research and educate us on sustainability and equality. The goal is neither money nor power, but a sustainable and healthy world that we can be proud of.

"The ultimate measure of a man is not where he stands in moments of comfort and convenience, but where he stands at times of challenge and controversy."
-Martin Luther King Jr

Although it may seem easier to ignore these issues, it is hugely irresponsible of our governments and corporations to do so for their own individual gains. An analogy for this, borrowed and adapted from Kip Andersen[264], is that we all live in a big house together. The main issue is the house is on fire. However, the people profiting from the fire are telling us we shouldn't be concerned and we should focus our energy on making our beds, dusting the mantelpiece and cleaning the windows.

Our current set of crises could force us to unite, regardless of our narrative-based divisions such as race, gender and nationality. Our systems should be embracing this opportunity.

## Freedom Protection

It is interesting to look at freedom with regards to laws. To break this down let's start with one that we all, generally speaking, agree on. It is–and should continue to be–against the law to kill someone. On a global level, all countries have at some point introduced this. And of course, it is a useful and healthy law. If you kill somebody, you are encroaching on their freedom and their right to live.

Now let's look at a more debatable scenario. One where what's right and wrong may not be so apparent. Let's suppose there are two people waiting at a bus stop in a public place. It's raining and as neither person wants to get wet they both share the fairly confined area of the public bus shelter. One of them starts to smoke but the other asks them to stop. Who would have more rights in this situation? Is the person who smokes encroaching on the non-smoker's freedom and the right to clean air, not smelling of smoke and so on? Or, is the person who is asking the smoker to stop encroaching on their freedom to smoke in a public place?

As neither situation creates long term side-effects (in small doses), you could say that it should remain excluded from national or global law and it is down to the discretion of the individual. However, with undebatable encroachments of freedom and unsustainable negative acts, we could say that they merit a hard line in the sand and a clear law.

What is interesting about this is that unsustainable behaviour such as air, water and soil pollution, and rapid resource depletion are often seen as down to our discretion. However, these actions can have long-term, negative side-effects, and in many cases can be fatal. In fact, they can kill far more people than an illegal gun shot.

Should our right to consume or pursue profit be allowed to override another's right to clean air, clean water or a healthy food supply? Do we view these crimes as victimless as we cannot always see the victim?

The Earth Stats service and Earth Score and Fair Trade labelling suggested in the Free System won't tell us how to live, but it does provide us with the tools to make well-informed decisions. It provides us with the information to protect our freedoms and act responsibly. Similar to the health warnings on a packet of cigarettes, you are still able to exercise your free will, but at least you are aware of the consequences.

In our current system, not only are malpractices hidden, they are actively protected by an increasing number of tactics. In 2016, a filmmaker was arrested for documenting a pipeline protest, with charges that could lead to 45 years in prison[265]. This is not the sole case where those who aim to spread awareness have been silenced, nor is it the most severe.

Throughout the world activists are regularly murdered. In 2015, a report by Global Witness documented 185 killings, and there are likely to be a great deal more that go unreported due to the often remote locations[266]. Some of the worst-hit countries were Colombia with 26 deaths, the Philippines with 33 deaths, and Brazil with 50 deaths[267]. The deaths are often related to conflicts over logging, fossil fuels and agricultural practices[268].

Brave people trying to protect their communities, the environment, and future generations are being killed and our governments are failing to protect them. Among those killed were the family of Michelle Campos, in an attack that drove 3,000 indigenous people from their homes[269].

"We get threatened, vilified and killed for standing up to the mining companies on our land and the paramilitaries that protect them … My father, grandfather, and school teacher were just three of countless victims. We know the murderers–they are still walking free in our community. We are dying and our government does nothing to help us."
-Michelle Campos

I believe the public would not support the companies involved if they knew the truth. The natural resources are often captured in remote parts of the world, which can further facilitate covert activities. There is a growing amount of companies with blood on their hands. No amount of profit justifies such abuse of human rights. None of these actions should remain hidden from the consumer. No one person's 'right to consume' should justify suffering or irreparable harm to the planet.

"Truth is treason in an empire of lies."
-George Orwell

Our target should be full transparency, protection, and a practical limit of consumption. Therefore the goal within our hypothetical system should be to not just use one planet's worth of renewable resources, but less than one, enabling us to leave behind greater opportunities for our children. Rather than taking as much as possible and pushing the limits of sustainability, we could be striving to create a symbiotic relationship with our environments; where we also give back and improve the planet for future generations. The target is not simply survival, but improved health and a brighter future. You wouldn't steal food from your child's dinner plate, but are we inadvertently doing this everyday through unsustainable and avoidable practices?

"When I think of what could be, I visualize an organization of people, committing to a purpose, and the purpose is doing no harm."
-Ray Anderson


It is important to clarify that a push for sustainability is not encroaching on our freedoms, it is protecting them. In addition to this we could further protect our collective freedoms through autonomous communities and self-governed, local projects. We will explore these in the next chapter as well as our new economies and what daily life could look like within our Free System.

"We who believe in freedom cannot rest until it comes."
-Ella Baker

CHAPTER 8

# ECONOMIES

What could replace money?

"It is not for me to change you. The question is, how can I be of service to you without diminishing your degrees of freedom?"
-Richard Buckminster Fuller

Within the Free System, we can collectively and democratically decide on decisions that affect us as a whole. These issues will be researched and the problems will be solved as soon as possible. However, matters outside of communal issues, such as the way you choose to live your life, can be defined by you. A potential mistake with many progressive movements is telling people how to live their daily lives. This is not the objective of a Free System. The goal is to explore sustainable and fair frameworks where people can lead their own lives and ultimately become far more autonomous. While we need broad guidelines and practical restrictions, we can't allow ourselves to become a dictatorship. Imposing ways of life on people creates wars and terrorism because it often forces somebody to completely redesign their lifestyle, culture and traditions.

Within a Free System you are free to create and build communities that are in line with your values. Provided you are responsible, sustainable and fair, you should not be limited or constricted with your personal rights in the

119

pursuit of happiness. As a collective we will intervene when someone's human rights are being violated but, providing that no one is suffering and the actions are sustainable, we will respect their rights to freedom as this is an opportunity that we, ourselves, would equally like to be awarded. Ultimately this system embraces the concept of treating others as you would like to be treated, in a framework that protects and ensures sustainable decisions.

# The Economy of Time

"A true revolution of values will soon cause us to question the fairness and justice of many of our past and present policies."
-Martin Luther King Jr.

Our global currencies and markets are often inhumane and unfair. Why have we come to accept that one hour's worth of work can be worth far less in another country, even within the same sector, with the same skills and using the exact same resources? The length of an hour is the same in any country on Earth. If you want something, contribute your time. No system can be fairer and simpler than this. This is the essence of our hypothetical new economy: a shift from money to a currency of time.

"Time is the most powerful resource in the world; it is an incredible equaliser between all humans. No matter who we are, no matter where we're from, no matter our background, we are all given exactly the same hours in a day."
-Sash Milne

In our current system you can use your age, race, gender, nationality, family's name or any number of non-chosen traits, to take more than your fair share of resources. A new system could offer us the chance to finally free ourselves from this cruel and competitive battle.

"Your time is equal to my time, no questions."
-Sash Milne


Within a Free System it is in everyone's best interest to ensure that their community is well-fed, happy and healthy as this would foster a reliable and effective workforce. As everyone's voice carries equal weight we'd all be pushing for an advanced and accessible education system to ensure a well-informed democracy. A loss for one doesn't have to be viewed as a gain for another. We can collectively grow as a whole in an enriching system of contribution.


"We are in this together, these aren't just words, the truth is, at some level, when you hurt, when your children hurt, I hurt."
-Bernie Sanders


As Senator Bernie Sanders noted, "It's very easy to turn our backs on kids who are hungry or veterans who are sleeping out in the street. We develop a psyche which says I don't have to worry about them, all I'm going to worry about is myself. I need to make another 5 billion dollars."[270]

If we stop and think about our current system, we can see we are moving further and further away from collaboration, compassion, and contribution. In our modern capitalist system it could be a financial benefit to you if another worker is unhealthy, uneducated or dealing with any number of issues, as this could lead to you obtaining a promotion and a higher salary. Similarly, it is clear that in our current system a corporation can financially benefit if a company that produces the same product as them goes out of business. In a system of contribution however, we all benefit from our collective success. No longer will we have to live in a dog-eat-dog world.

It is not sustainable or ethical to take and take and not contribute. Within a capitalist system, someone who has inherited a vast amount of wealth by any number of means may spend the rest of their life without contributing to their community. In fact their 'contribution' may well be inequality.

"I am opposing a social order in which it is possible for one man who does absolutely nothing that is useful to amass a fortune of hundreds of millions of dollars, while millions of men and women who work all the days of their lives secure barely enough for a wretched existence."
-Eugene V. Debs

While many in our current system may appear to benefit from taking more than their fair share, I believe that all of us could become happier and healthier with a time-based, contribution economy.

"When we do the right thing and try to treat people with respect and dignity, when we say that child who is hungry is my child. I think that we are more human when we do that, than when we say this whole world is me, I need more, I don't care about anybody else."
-Bernie Sanders

A system of contribution, communication and collaboration could foster a healthy environment which values the things that we naturally value. This could lead to less repression and less regret as we'd focus on what really matters in life.

When palliative nurse Bronnie Ware began to record the regrets mentioned by her patients moments before they passed away, she noticed common recurring themes during their final moments of clarity. They didn't regret not buying certain items, not working more hours, nor failing to become rich and famous. The most common regrets were free and involved being true to themselves and maintaining honest connections with other people. The four most common regrets are[271]:

1. Not living a life true to my values.
2. Working too hard and not prioritising time with family.

3. Suppressing feelings.

4. Not staying in touch with friends.

Ware's findings are also echoed in the studies of Professors Kirk Brown and Tim Kasser which revealed that those who prioritise intrinsic values such as self-development, relationships, and community are happier than those who focus on extrinsic values such as status, image and money[272].

"We must rapidly begin the shift from a thing-oriented society to a person-oriented society."
-Martin Luther King Jr.

A system of contribution is one which learns from our previous mistakes and prioritises social values. This is very different from our current political systems and therefore it could be confused with a pipe-dream. However, as we'll see later, there are various communities, movements and even active political parties that promote and facilitate a moneyless contribution economy. But first, let's take a slightly closer look at how a time-based contribution system could work at a national level.

We could provide people with different ways to live and structure their lives.

Community
Should you wish to live in a more self-reliant community, yourself and a group of people can choose to collaborate and find a plot of land to create a new settlement. As long as you are sustainable and don't negatively affect those around you, you are free to do as you wish. Should you need additional resources, you are free to trade with the country. Alternatively, you may wish to create a federation of communities to open up larger trading networks.

You are free to move or change situation at any time; likewise you are free to remain as part of a community. Indigenous groups or current sustainable settlements are treated equally as any other community and are allowed to live in peace, free at last from the force of capitalism. The government will be open to receive applications regarding new plots of land where individuals or communities would like to settle. As the government will be transparent, the criteria of a sustainable plot will be published for all to see, critique and improve. It will use scientific, impartial measurements to determine a sustainability value. Field researchers would give each settlement application an Earth Score. Anything below 1 will be accepted. As our technologies develop with the right incentives, it will become easier to be sustainable and self-sufficient. With a redirection of focus from money and power to our collective goals, we could see huge breakthroughs in sustainable and ethical technology.

Country

If you wish to remain closer to the existing model, you can choose to work as part of the country. The country will be comprised of organisations, public services and community projects that contribute to the country–including the government. All of these places of work will contribute to the people and can be directed through democratic votes. There will be no unemployment as you can always work for your country. Everyone in the country contributes. As a member of the country contribution force you have free access to anything you need.

International Trading

International trading is open to communities and countries. Any trading made between countries will be fully transparent and led by the people. We aim to help as many people as possible and therefore hope to build free and open trading networks between all countries. All countries can benefit from an international market of resources if we are transparent, fair and sustainable. Anything that we learn that can be freely shared will be available to all. We strive to make a global shift to contribution and collaboration as this can provide us all with a safe and abundant future.

Co-ops

Rather than rulers or dictators, we hope to see representatives from the communities who can communicate with other groups. Self-led communities can form federations with other communities should they wish to contribute or collaborate on projects. This is similar to that of the Iroquois, a Native American Confederacy comprised of six nations[*]. Although they frequently worked as a collective, there was no one ruler and no one nation encroached on the other's freedom.

# A Day in the Life

"If we change money, we'll change the world."
-Mick Taylor

## The Country Farmer

To explore a Free System in greater detail, let's follow a hypothetical case study: a 40-year-old male farmer who works for his country. He lives in a city and has a mixed social group of country contributors. He commutes to work on a free train and works for two hours. As he is part of his union, he has greater input in how his workplace is run, and they have collectively decided to have an optional, hour long, communal lunch break. He then works for a further two hours and takes the free train home. He is then free to do as he wishes with his spare time.

When he goes shopping he takes what he needs for free and leaves, with only rational limits applied. No money is used as currency as his contribution acts like a free credit card. His contribution card is proof of his role within the country and he is therefore entitled to the contributions of others. He goes back to his rent-free apartment. His focus is not individual gain but contributing to those around him and forming authentic connections. Work is

---

[*] The Mohawk, Onondaga, Oneida, Cayuga, Seneca, and Tuscarora

viewed holistically. His work empowers others to eat for free. Similarly, because the builder went to work, others have a place to live. It is a symbiotic relationship. No one is exploiting anybody as the work is evenly distributed through the universal measurement of contribution time.

The people can collectively decide how much everyone contributes. No one is forced to work more than others and no one is viewed above anyone else. After unpacking his free shopping the farmer goes to a community leisure centre. Not only are the resources free but, more importantly, he has the time, energy, and health to enjoy it. Later, he dines with his friends at a free sustainable restaurant and no one has to worry about dividing the bill. In fact, at no point in his life will he have to worry about money.

A Community Member

Let's assume our hypothetical community member is a 28-year-old female. She is a carpenter within a (mostly) self-sufficient community of 150 people. As she primarily works for the community, her hours and responsibilities could be decided by a community vote. It could also be decided another way as the community are free to develop their own infrastructure. In this example she has her own workshop where she works her own hours. The community requests certain items and she helps to make them. For food and other products she goes to the free community market. Similar to the country farmer, she has a symbiotic relationship with her community.

As her community don't have a water well or solar panels, they also contribute to the country in exchange for free water and electricity. They could also trade with other communities, but they choose to trade with the country. In exchange for this, she works the equivalent of 4 contribution hours every two months for the country.

# Satisfyingly Simple

"Though the problems of the world are becoming increasingly complex, the solutions remain embarrassingly simple."

-Bill Mollison

There could be no rent, no taxes, no middle-men, no invoices, no loans, no hidden costs, no mortgages, no bills, no bonds, no debts, no market crashes, no bailouts, no million-dollar bonuses, no offshore accounts, no interest rates, no small print, no sign-up fee, no commission fee, no legal fee, no cancellation fee, no owners, no banks and no money. You contribute to your country and community, and in exchange gain access to the shared resources.

Just imagine all of the useless, unhealthy jobs that we could get rid of. Imagine how much our new industries could contribute.

In an interview with Owen Jones, political author Rutger Bregman noted that "since the 1980s we've seen a huge amount of new jobs that don't really need to exist."[273] He also notes how we are stuck in a 19th century mindset, where we have to constantly find ways to work for money. He suggests that, "We need to rethink what work actually is, because there is so much work that's unpaid that is incredibly valuable: volunteer work, caring for our kids, caring for our elderly."[274]

Whilst we cannot deny the importance of the work of volunteers, charities and food banks all around the world, they do also act as further warning signs that our current political systems don't work. Our governments shouldn't rely on the goodwill of the public to prop up a system that fails to look after them.

We often mistake profit as a sign that the public needed a service or commodity. So many jobs in today's society were created solely because an opportunity to make money became available. In reality, working and contribution are not always inherently linked in our current systems.

In 2015, Yougov revealed that "37% of working British adults say their job is not making a meaningful contribution to the world."[275] And according to a recent worldwide report, only 13% of people actually like their job[276]. The majority of us are not working for contribution nor passion, but to earn money in order to afford a living. Through a new system we could remove useless jobs, and transform the ideology of working to make money into contributing to society.

In our current system a company often seeks to create something of use, make money, or both. Once you remove the monetary aspect you are free to focus on authentically helping those around you. Work could transform into an actual labour of love as it is your way of contributing. This could help us put the heart and soul into our workplaces. We shouldn't be in a situation where we have to choose between an honest job or having enough. A noble way of life is doing the best you can, not causing harm, and helping others. Our systems should facilitate this.

"People want to serve some greater good ... They find it impossible to respect themselves if they are giving more of their time helping to produce and sell products or services that do not correspond to deeper human values."
-Jacob Needleman

Can we at least dare to think big? We are often in a catch-22 where we can be criticised for either not offering sufficient solutions or offering ideas that are too ambitious. There is great value in exploring brand-new systems, even purely as a way to remain open-minded or to see things from a fresh perspective. We need new ideas. We need to explore new paths. While these may seem like utopian concepts, why should that be a bad thing? A utopia is an ideal state. Shouldn't our political systems try to facilitate ideal scenarios? Our hypothetical system is an ideal state using the knowledge and resources that we already have.

## Contribution Card

"The only thing that any of us really need for true and lasting social change is time."
-Sash Milne

Do we value money over humanity? If we adjust to an immoral system what do we become? Can we reverse a lifetime of harmful traditions? Can we shift from what is 'best' for the individual to what is best for us all? Can we leave behind the battle for possessions and status, and even the battle with our own egos?

Just because we use money now, that shouldn't mean that we have to use it indefinitely. I am not suggesting taking on the banks nor fighting the biggest private corporations. I am suggesting we explore new currencies, where we use time as a tool of contribution.

"We don't need to kneel to the banks. We can stand for what we really value in each other and we can start by losing our delusions about money, working for real reform, trying real alternatives."
-Jem Bendell

Just to clarify, this doesn't mean that we replace dollars for 'time dollars'. With a full contribution economy, we can evolve beyond money. This will also help us to move past ideological barriers and the concept of ownership and material 'success'. Our hypothetical contribution card doesn't have digital credit or even a numerical amount on it. It simply proves that you are either part of the contribution pool, working towards being part of the contribution pool, or unable to contribute.

And if you cannot contribute due to an illness or whatever it may be, then you will be provided with the care that you need as this is how we'd like to be treated.

"If we are going to find a new approach to the money question, it will have to enable us to bring time back into our lives."
-Jacob Needleman

We can collectively decide a reasonable amount of minimum hours of contribution required to maintain a sustainable and fair society. We could begin with 6 hours, which is implemented in Sweden[277], as it was shown to greatly increase health as well as efficiency[278]. However, with a more collaborative model, less useless jobs and less unemployment, that number could decrease further, especially as we redefine our notions of value and purpose. If you are in a self-reliant, sustainable community, the number of hours you work may vary. In either scenario, we would be working for ourselves and our compatriots within an ethical and sustainable system.

"I think that it is about time that we award the better impulses, to care for each other, to come to each other's rescue, to stand up for what's right, to oppose what's wrong."
-Edgar Cahn

Your contribution card would give you access to things that were otherwise monetized as well as things that were otherwise available through taxation, such as health care and education. As we start from scratch and re-examine the existing frameworks, we can set new standards for things such as paid annual leave. Perhaps you would start with 36 days 'paid' annual leave, which is currently practiced in countries such as Finland, France, and Iceland.

The contribution card doesn't fix inequality with a wage cap nor an increased minimum wage. It empowers us to evolve beyond the notion of private wealth, not towards a basic 'allowance', but a dignified shared economy.

This wouldn't be a system where people do nothing, as that wouldn't make sense; neither would it be an economy where others could stockpile far more than they would ever need, as that also doesn't make sense. You couldn't bribe governments with a time currency nor could you stockpile huge masses of wealth as there are only a certain numbers of hours in the day. The currency of time is naturally limited. We can shift from money motivation to community motivation.

This is not a new concept, but our natural way. Hunter-gatherers were egalitarian by nature; they 'worked' for the whole tribe with very little wealth differentiation[279]. Small societies are inherently against isolated power as well as those who don't contribute as this not only causes conflict, it is incredibly unsustainable. Our ancestors were quick to keep these kinds of people in check as they compromise the unit. Greed and isolated power is bad for us, our community and our environment; therefore, it was not tolerated within a tribe economy, nor is it facilitated in our new time-based economy.

If our national budgets were only limited to the scientific measurement of available time and sustainable resources then we could see much-needed breakthroughs. Finally our systems could embrace common sense. Products would be healthy and either last for a certain number of years or be incredibly resource efficient to recycle. We wouldn't have to invent jobs for the sake of it. We wouldn't have to continue harmful practices. Our politicians could finally promote less consumption. We could have rational and preventative systems. We could embrace common sense rather than business sense. We could live authentic compassionate lives.

"Cultural shifts only occur when the vast majority of the population decides to redefine that which has always been assumed as a given, like the model of success, like the value of time, like what it is that truly makes people happy."
-Sash Milne

This isn't a complete system, rather a hypothetical set of ideas, a chance to reimagine what we might see as unchangeable constants. It is certainly not the only option, and there are multiple ways that you could expand and develop some of these concepts.

# CHAPTER 9
# UPGRADES

How could a Free System evolve?

T he basic blueprint starts with our founding pillars of sustainability and equality–a solid foundation, measurable through scientific rigour, that maintains a zero tolerance to unsustainable acts and prevents systems that only serve a few. It is then safe to focus on the remaining collective goals: community, happiness, ethics and freedom. In service of these goals we explored various tools and frameworks such as Earth Stats, Earth Score, embracing controversial challenges, localised politics, independent communities, direct democracy, and a time-based, contribution economy. This aims to be a simple modular system that fosters community resilience and deeper connections through a pay-it-forward system of reciprocity.

We've recently seen some more of the consequences of isolated power bubble up to the surface with cases such as that of Harvey Weinstein[*], and perhaps we have only seen the tip of the iceberg. Isolated power can mutate us and remove us from community and compassion. A Free System is ultimately about a dissolution of power and the birth of a brand-new value system.

---

[*] One of the most influential film producers Harvey Weinstein has received numerous sexual misconduct allegations where he is reported to have grossly abused his power.

"The current philosophy says that money is everything, profit is god."
-Akala


If we take the analogy of a rusty old car in desperate need of repair, there comes a point where it is beyond help. It can become unsafe and it may not have been built in a way that makes full use of current knowledge. In this scenario you will only reach full potential if you start from the beginning and build a brand-new frame.

We could add restrictions and amendments to our current systems, but this could be a waste of the potential upgrades that we could receive with a brand-new system; not just one that protects the remaining healthy environments but actively creates them. A new system could enable us to drive away from divisive ideologies towards authentic connections. Daily life could remind us that it is our unity that provides us with the lifestyle that we have democratically chosen. A Free System acknowledges our current crimes—exploitation of people and the planet—and adopts a zero tolerance to slavery, injustice and dictatorships. It is deeply immoral for our politicians to ignore the problems of globalisation and continue a harrowing lack of respect for the global south. A Free System is one that we could be proud of and it is just the beginning.

One of the most fundamental aspects of a Free System is that it is free to evolve and adapt to situations. Ultimately these variations would be decided by the people who form that contribution pool and will vary greatly depending on needs, cultures and resources. With the benefit of supporting free independent communities alongside a national system, we can continuously study alternative solutions. They can act as open-source idea incubators. They can cultivate progress. They could ensure that we remain open-minded.

"Real knowledge is to know the extent of one's ignorance"
-Confucius

We are the result of our environments and the product of generations before us. This means we are by nature compromised by our limited perspective. We must continue to question ourselves, our systems and our environments. Homosexuals were once sent to be 'cured', the right to vote was once limited to a single gender, and the colour of a person's skin could dictate whether they could take a seat on the bus. Isn't it presumptuous to assume there aren't a great deal more immoral acts that we could have become immune to? Beyond the growing environmental damage and the increasing levels of inequality, are there injustices beyond our compromised lens?

It is our turn to identify what should be removed from our societies and adopt a zero tolerance to it. It is our time to set new standards to the best of our abilities. However, we should be conscious of our limitations and remain open-minded and humble, and thus create a more malleable modular framework for future generations. They may develop tools and techniques beyond our current understanding. It's when systems become unchallengeable and ideas become dogmatic that we halt. We can embrace critique and evolution. We can leave the book open.

## Rights to Revise

As we continue to democratically evolve our system, we can redefine governmental responsibilities, human rights and societal needs. A useful starting point can be to study the hierarchy of human needs, as outlined by pioneering psychologist Abraham Maslow[280]:

· Physiological: air, food, water and rest.
· Safety: security, health and well-being.
· Social belonging: intimacy, friendship and family.
· Esteem: respect, happiness and a feeling of accomplishment.
· Self-actualization: learning, fulfilment and helping others.

It is useful to reflect on how our current system facilitates or impedes the fulfilment of our essential human needs and how systemic improvements could help. We can then redefine the responsibilities of the government and set new human rights. You may break it down into something similar to the following:

Government responsibilities:
· Create and uphold a just democracy
· Establish and maintain ecological sustainability
· Maintain full transparency
· Protect the people from corruption and exploitation
· Respect the freedom of the people
· Allow the public to develop their own communities
· Protect the rights of the people

Human rights:
· Democracy
· Shelter
· Healthy food and clean water
· Clean atmosphere
· Employment
· Education
· Health care
· Protection
· Leisure time
· Freedom

In addition to governmental duties and human rights, we can also redefine many practices and institutes, such as our companies, our professions, technology and health care. By starting from the ground up and remaining open-minded, we could see massive system upgrades.

# The Jobs People Don't Want To Do

"Normal is getting dressed in clothes that you buy for work, driving through traffic in a car that you are still paying for, in order to get to a job that you need so you can pay for the clothes, car and the house that you leave empty all day in order to afford to live in it."
-Ellen Goodman

In our current system there are many jobs that no one wants to do, but people are nonetheless pressured into completing these tasks. They often have to work long hours and are paid poorly. Let's take a look at how we can approach this controversial subject differently. Let's take the scenario where the public have voted that they want clean streets, but no one wants the job of cleaning them.

Firstly, we would assess the root causes of the issue to see if we could prevent the streets becoming dirty in the first place. Let's pretend that we couldn't prevent it, even though we probably could. Secondly, we would look to technology: can we automate the task? Let's pretend the job cannot be automated, again, even though it likely could. If there was no other option, in this scenario the public would face a choice: either don't have the service, or, if you want to keep the service, everybody in the community shares that role. Rather than one person forced into doing a job they don't like doing, every single day, everybody would do a small portion. The task would be divided and evenly distributed. No one person would feel shame as everyone is in the same situation. Everybody could do ten minutes of street cleaning every six months as a community contribution rather than an individual sacrificing an unfulfilled lifetime.

Why should we expect others to do things that we wouldn't want to do ourselves? Together we can create a world that truly serves us all. We can empower others to obtain a quality of life that we would like to be awarded.

136

Our political systems could address our internal and external needs. All our jobs could have a true communal purpose. We could have more autonomy at work and could be given the opportunity through open-source education to be a master in that task. Our systems could, therefore, satisfy our psychological needs as outlined by Professors Edward Deci and Richard Ryan: "to feel autonomous, to feel competent and to feel related to others."[281]

Just to clarify, I still believe that people will likely have one area of expertise. This is just an idea of a new way to tackle and evenly distribute the remaining unwanted tasks. And indeed it may well be a moot point, as not only do I feel we could automate these jobs, I also feel that if we become proud of our environments and ways of life these things won't happen in the first place. Littering is very much a symptom of a disenfranchised population who don't feel a strong sense of community. The more you sacrifice for something, often, the more you value it. If your primary 'job' is to contribute to your community, you will feel deeply invested and you will value it much more.

# Technology

There are some things in life to which we don't yet know the cure, and there are some things where we know the cure, but lack the resources. We currently have the resources and knowledge to help a lot of people, but we have the human-created boundary of money. We have a total acceptance of privately controlled and stockpiled wealth, which can act as a commercial and political blockade.

Everybody on this planet could have free energy for life, in so far as there is certainly not a lack of an abundant sustainable resource. The sun is a near perfect sphere of hot plasma that burns at twenty-seven million degrees Fahrenheit. If the sunlight that touches Texas were harvested for energy, it would generate 300 times the total power output of all the power plants in the world[282]. And if we consider this technology could be installed on unused rooftops and in uninhabitable deserts, it seems unbelievable that we are still drilling for oil.

In the 2016 documentary *Before the Flood*, inventor and engineer Elon Musk revealed that we would only need 100 Tesla-built Gigafactories* to transition the whole world to sustainable energy[283]. However, Tesla cannot afford to build that many. As a result, we risk missing out on many of the benefits this technology could bring.

We will continue to pollute the planet, drain non-renewable resources, invade other countries, and invest in unsustainable and temporary solutions as we are blocked from progressing and evolving. We have become poisoned, limited and perhaps enslaved by something that we have created. A new system could remove artificial barriers and legacy narratives. We could go right into solving our collective problems as soon as possible.

In addition to increased transparency and removing blockades, technology could also greatly increase our sense of democracy. We could monitor governmental meetings and choose to vote on more decisions if we wish. We don't need money to organise our lives. Just as our current global challenges can help us unite, open-source instant communication can help us organise ourselves in an ethically justifiable manner. We could evolve the current practice of voting with your dollar to an optimised democratic electronic vote: open democracy. There will be no elite entry ticket. No amount of money should be able to increase your 'democratic' vote.

Removing money does not mean removing markets. We can create new markets. Ones with vital limits and regulations applied. Ones where the people can democratically guide the process. Where the public can prioritise the development of things that serve them rather than exploit them.

Due to the modular nature of a free and evolving system, we could vote to change specific areas at a time, with each option backed by peer-reviewed studies that are translated effectively to the public. A quick test could ensure that the voter fully understands what they are voting for and transparent communication could convey the consequences. Rather than the current, highly restrictive two-party system, we could unite and shape a system that

---

* A Gigafactory is a large scale, energy self-reliant battery, construction factory.

works for the people and the planet. We could also expand this further and vote for products and corporations that we'd like to see.

While technology can assist us in many ways, we'll have to be cautious of leaning on it too heavily as a quick fix. Much like 'treating' depression with a pill, if we rely on gadgets to clean up our mistakes we may leave root causes untreated. We might continue bad habits and inadvertently cut off opportunities through a false sense of security. We may fix the symptoms but not the mindset that created the problems.

If we continue to lose vital micro-organisms in our soil we will be forced to invent new farming techniques. This could seem like progression but would perhaps lead to less options than if we applied preventative measures today.

In short, technology can help us, even in the preventative stages, but it would be unwise to continue harmful practices 'safe' in the knowledge that we can always reverse the consequences. We have to be careful not to become dependent on technology. This could greatly decrease our freedom. As it stands today, we have sufficient resources for an abundant future. Protecting these should be a priority.

# Health

In our supermarkets we often have a healthy food section. However, this begs the question: what does that make the rest of the store? Our current systems do not prioritise mental or physical health, and we greatly suffer in our often relentless pursuit of money. This can create a highly inefficient cyclical pattern.

"They lose their health to make money and then lose their money to restore their health."
-James J. Lachard

A labourer may have to work extra shifts to pay for a chiropractor, when overwork was the root cause of their injury. Parents may choose to live outside of the city and commute to work in order to save money to support their family. However, the extra two-hour commute decreases the amount of quality time they can spend together. Incidentally, a recent report by the Guardian highlighted that a two-hour commute is the reality for nearly 4 million UK workers, largely due to the cost of living[284].

"The system should serve our happiness, strength, and health."
-Wim Hoff

In our current system, many of us are accidentally harming ourselves and the people around us. We are commuting greater distances. We spend a huge part of our day under fluorescent lights, staring into a glowing screen. We're eating unnatural processed chemicals that we can't even pronounce the names of, let alone recognise in a line-up. We are sitting more and moving less. We are breathing in polluted air. And we are often in isolating and stressful conditions. Brief standing breaks can be filled with the temporary highs of sugar, caffeine, and nicotine. Millions of people adopt the unhealthy and incredibly inefficient culture of living for the weekend to offset the daily grind. We are tolerating, endorsing and even funding literal cancer causers. We are increasingly removed from our natural and healthy state. We are no longer indigenous to our environments. We are overfeeding but malnourished, overprotected but weak, and somehow we are both sanitised yet deeply infected.

As we increasingly become static consumers, we all, in every sense, pay the price. Accordingly statistics reveal that our children's health is in danger: rates for teenage suicide are rapidly climbing[285], childhood obesity is now 10 times higher than it was in the 70s[286], and depression among adolescents and young adults has increased by 37%[287].

"What greater indictment of a system could there be than an epidemic of mental illness?"

-George Monbiot

Our increasingly unnatural environments could also help to explain the rapidly rising cases of diabetes[288] and cardiovascular diseases[289], as well as the plummeting sperm counts in Western countries[290]. In fact, if we look at America, which currently has the largest economy[291], we can see the real price of 'winning' capitalism. More than one-third of American adults are obese[292] and 50% have one or more chronic health condition[293]. When for the 'leading' country, daily lifestyles, products and the general environment could be classified as the biggest threat to national security, then we have to acknowledge that the system is incredibly flawed. Not only does it seemingly ignore the root causes but it funds, creates, promotes, and rewards them.

When we solely treat symptoms we miss out on a wealth of opportunities. Some issues require holistic treatments with reforms in many areas such as corporate restrictions, promoting new lifestyles and updating school curriculums. We should be very suspicious of quick fixes and scapegoats. The culture of symptom treating can in many cases exacerbate issues, not only because they allow root causes to grow but also because they allow those affected to further endure scenarios they would otherwise be forced to tackle.

When you treat the symptoms you limit yourself to that single issue. However, when you attack the root cause you have a chance at fixing a vast number of issues that may appear unrelated but are in fact deeply connected. As symptom treatments can last an entire lifetime, they can be incredibly profitable; therefore, unfortunately, they become increasingly common within capitalism.

An example of which is Abilify, an antipsychotic that quickly became the best-selling drug in the U.S.[294]. It was heavily marketed as helping with depression, something that affects millions of Americans. Not only does the drug not tackle a root cause, its side effects can include nausea, impaired vision, tiredness, weight gain and trouble sleeping[295], things that can actually perpetuate the problem. In the U.S. there has been a 400% increase in the use of antidepressants among all age groups[296], and through intense marketing Abilify became one of the many go-to symptom 'treatments'.

However, it doesn't have to be this way. There are mounting scientific studies proving that free and easy-to-implement lifestyle changes can heal or prevent numerous health issues, from stress, anxiety and depression to arthritis and cancer. Increasing evidence is showing that heat and cold exposure[297] [298], diets with fewer processed foods[299], regular exercise[300], less interaction with technology[301], more socialising[302] and even periods of fasting[303] can have a profound impact on our health, resilience, happiness, quality of life and life longevity. These are things that our ancestors would have done naturally, based on their environment and circumstance. So much of modern life is in conflict with what our bodies have evolved to do.

Somewhere along the way mankind got side-tracked. In a big way. We went from working outside for our families and communities to working in boxes for corporations. Our ways of life became increasingly driven by corporate profits: what we eat, where we work, how we act, our laws, our hobbies and even our beliefs.

If you don't eat certain food for your entire life and then binge on it, you can become ill. Likewise if you don't do any exercise and then start going to the gym twice a day, you will likely experience physical pain as you adapt. This is useful to remember when reflecting upon our current lifestyles. For over 99% of our time on Earth we ate only organic natural food, we did regular outdoor activities and we lived in tightly-knit communities. What many of us are experiencing now is a gigantic shock to the system. Accordingly, our leading health professionals are currently recommending actions that try to counteract the effects of consumerism.

Unfortunately, it seems unthinkable for our current system to promote less consumption, even if it will save our lives and protect vital natural resources. Instead we are sold the idea that we should live a life of consumption and then pay to treat the symptoms. In essence, we are consuming to treat the symptoms of over-consumption. We are treating fire with fire.

The 'buy-now-think-later' mentality is evident through marketing tag lines such as "have it your way", "be more", "just do it" and "what happens in Vegas stays in Vegas." This further fosters the idea to consume as much as you want and promotes the myth that there are no consequences. This mentality causes great suffering; however, it also creates incredibly fertile ground for a rapidly growing GDP—the governmental score card.

"Taking food's place on the shelves has been an unending stream of food-like substitutes, some seventeen thousand new ones every year."
-Michael Pollan

We're sending people into jobs we know take decades off their life, as well as dramatically decreasing quality of life. And as we discover new healthy routines and diets, we know that many people can neither afford the time nor financial costs to implement them. This is truly heart-breaking and, worse still, it can further promote the dog-eat-dog 'rather them than me' mentality. When I lose motivation or become overwhelmed, I often think of the life that many could be living. When I see seas of mentally and physically unwell people and I know there are tried and tested solutions, I find the strength to increase my efforts.

Imagine if we could ask our leading scientists to develop the best diets and lifestyles for our health, happiness and sustainability without the distraction of money, without the need to increase consumption. Unfortunately, many of our leading scientists, who may have been in higher education for over a decade, are having to focus their research on profit-making endeavours. They are compromised by private funders and the influence of their own financial needs.

Our health care professionals are fighting against our processed foods and sedentary lifestyles; our leading psychologists are fighting an epidemic of stress, addictions and depression; and many of our leading technologists are focusing on ways to obtain more clicks on web-based advertising. Too frequently, important breakthroughs are underfunded and not prioritised. What if our products and gadgets were designed to reduce depression, anxiety and sickness? What if our pharmaceutical companies were searching for cures and not customers?

There are many health upgrades we could benefit from with a new system that tackles the root causes of our collective challenges, promotes preventative lifestyles and creates healthy environments.

## Representatives

"The time where people trust politicians, that's over, that era has passed."
-Russell Brand

To regain trust in our politicians within a new system, we could set up an independent watchdog committee who monitor their actions - a protective measure greatly lacking in our current system. This could include mandatory HR departments where employees can feel protected when they stand up to exploitation and reveal abuses of power. Our new government could be regularly rotated and it could be comprised of a true representation of the public. It could include people who work real jobs and have genuine life experience.

The majority of our current politicians are incredibly wealthy and yet they make decisions that affect the average person. They dictate and enforce a lousy minimum wage on the public and yet they often make ten times more[304]. They have likely never experienced a single day on the minimum amount[305].

"We have come to be one of the worst ruled, one of the most completely controlled and dominated governments in the civilised world, a government by the opinion and the duress of small groups of dominant men."
-Former U.S. President, Thomas Woodrow Wilson

Imagine how quickly things could change if politicians were on minimum wage, if they had to wait in line at hospitals dreading the costs, and if they had to start their careers with vast amounts of university debt. What if they had to work in a third-world factory and experience the labour that often fuels their own abundance? What if, when they leave politics, they were not offered advisory jobs for the corporations that they served while in office?

We have become accustomed to systems created by privileged people who often have little to no life experience. An extreme example of this is when we were ruled by kings. When the king died his son would be in charge; sometimes not even a teenager. We would then be forced into systems created by those with immense power and a lack of connection to real people, and little want for change.

"Nature knows no kings."
-Mark Samsonovich

## Compassion, Collaboration, and Connection

If a child doesn't see light in the early stages of development, they may never be able to see. This is a useful metaphor to discuss the importance of the environment in which we find ourselves. We are born with the capacity to be many things: brave or fearful, loving or hateful, kind or selfish. Our environments can help shape these attributes.

If there has just been an argument and someone tells a joke, you may not find it funny, whereas if you are in a relaxed environment and surrounded by friends you might laugh and smile. If a slow song is playing you may subconsciously walk slower. The layout of a room may influence where you choose to sit. Where we live can change our speech, where we went to school can change the way we think, and even the colour of a wall can affect our mood. As Bruce Lee once said, "You put water into a cup, it becomes the cup. Put it into a teapot, it becomes the teapot."[306] It is important to remind ourselves that our environments, while they may appear to support us, can also define, shape and limit us.

145

It is difficult to decouple environmental and biological factors with regards to what influences human behaviour. I believe it would be healthy to maintain an open mind and frequently experiment with new environments, new frameworks, lifestyles and ways of life. We may well be drastically limiting our potential due to a false sense of already 'knowing' what's best.

"Every man is a creature of the age in which he lives and few are able to raise themselves above the ideas of the time."
-Voltaire

One of the most famous experiments exploring the influence of our environments is the Rat Park experiment, conducted in the 70s by Professor Bruce Alexander[307]. It had previously been shown that a rat in a small empty cage provided with both pure water and water laced with drugs will eventually become addicted and end up killing itself via overdose. However, in the Rat Park experiment the rats had a larger and more stimulating, varied environment with activities and social communities. Subsequently, even when offered the same choice–water or drugged water–they chose the drug-free option. In fact, even when they introduced previously addicted rats, who had spent time in solitary confinement, they too chose the drug-free option.

As writer and journalist Johann Hari notes, "Human beings have a natural and innate need to bond, and when we're happy and healthy, we'll bond and connect with each other, but if you can't do that, because you're traumatized or isolated or beaten down by life, you will bond with something that will give you some sense of relief. Now, that might be gambling, that might be pornography, that might be cocaine, that might be cannabis, but you will bond and connect with something because that's our nature. That's what we want as human beings."[308]

Hari goes on to state that many of us could afford to drink vodka for the next 6 months, but we will choose not to as we already have bonds and connections we want to be present for. If we have purpose, pleasure and connections coming from elsewhere we won't seek an unhealthy and unsustainable alternative. As Hari notes, "The opposite of addiction is not sobriety. The opposite of addiction is connection." Compassionate and collaborative communities are fertile grounds for healthy and happy people.

"If we start to absorb the new evidence about addiction, I think we're going to have to change a lot more than our drug policies."
-Johann Hari

They say that your home is your castle, but why are we building a fortress? Why are we isolating ourselves and building barriers to community? People who leave the military often say they miss the camaraderie, as well as working outdoors, away from screens and towards a common goal[309]. People in sports teams often find it refreshing and fulfilling to contribute to something other than themselves and that they are not judged for what they own but rather their commitment to a unified cause[310]. And in times of national crisis people often say how they felt true connection to those around them as they united for something that really matters[311].

Many people grow tired of the cut-throat mentality of the modern world, in which we can lose our most important connections: with nature, with contribution and with each other. However, our current problems may force us to unite: global warming, water shortages, crop failures, bee colony collapses, soil degradation and so on. These challenges require collaboration and focusing on what really matters, even if it doesn't make business sense.

Seeing the many interconnections between us and how we are stronger when we are united will be a key catalyst for authentic systemic change. It is also what makes us human. As former political diplomat Carne Ross states, solitary confinement is punishment for a reason. Our relationships with each other gives us meaning as who are we without each other?[312] Who are we if we tolerate a system that allows others to suffer?

Interactions and connections define who we are as a race and we instinctively gravitate towards it. In fact, when given a choice of physical pain or isolation, social mammals will opt for the former.[313]

What is our current environment? Is it healthy? Does it promote collaboration, compassion, and genuine connections?

I don't view it as coincidence that a system dependant on increased consumption results in unsustainable and harmful outcomes. I don't view it as coincidence that as we deregulate corporations and cut social welfare that we see a growing gap between rich and poor. Nor do I see it as simple human weakness that in a system that promotes individualism and materialism we see a rise in mental health problems.

"When a flower doesn't bloom, you fix the environment in which it grows."
-Alexander Den Heijer

Our current systems can force us to compete with one another as they frequently reward selfishness and harmful acts. Our political systems can make us feel as though we can't make a difference. The media can render us fearful yet desensitised. Our adverts can make us feel inadequate and self-conscious. Our materialistic cultures and value on money can create individualistic lifestyles. We can start to view others as competition or inconveniences. With limited leisure time we could begin to treat socialising as appointments, something you have to book in advance and hopefully something you can fit neatly into your busy money-making schedule.

"This process of commodifying everything must end."
-Yanis Varoufakis

With the way our current system is arranged, there is forever the chance that someone may be hanging up a $20 million piece of artwork, and on the other side of that wall their neighbour may be crying due to financial concerns. You may beep and shout at someone on the way to work who was already going through a difficult time. It is far too easy to justify not helping in our current society and money plays a significant role. We often can't afford to give away free advice or free help; time is money. We might view giving to others with our ideas, money or time as taking a step down on a ladder, one we feel we must constantly climb. This mentality is evident in pessimistic expressions such as "Every man for himself" and "No good deed goes unpunished."

Too often we are in an anxious and reactive state. We need the space and time to think about the consequences of our actions, and to listen to and care for others. We need to meet in smaller groups and make genuine connections, moving beyond cocktail networking or superficial small talk. Many people are alone in society. We need healthy and clear communication. We need a system that promotes our positive attributes. One that facilitates kindness.

"It is evident that the form of government is best in which every man, whoever he is, can act best and live happily."
-Aristotle

Sadly, in our current system helping others is often not valued, and in some cases not even tolerated. In 2014, 90-year-old World War 2 veteran Arnold Abbott, who runs a non-profit group called Love Thy Neighbour, was arrested for feeding homeless people in Florida[314].

In 2015, Citylab revealed nearly one third of Americans say they have never interacted with their neighbours[315]. If we can't even connect with those next to us, how will we become engaged in the crimes that happen across the world?

A lack of community is inefficient at best. A block of apartments with 300 suites who lack community could have 300 hammers, 300 bike pumps and 300 cars. We can hugely reduce waste by thinking and acting as a collective. By redesigning the concept of ownership and moving towards open-source sharing models, we can greatly reduce our demand on the world's resources as well as decreasing our sense of isolation.

Self-reliant communities are particularly important for the future of our food. Even if you adopt a more sustainable diet and purchase only organic products, it is still incredibly inefficient to transport these products around the world. To remedy this, many people attempt the 100 Mile Diet, where you purchase from local farmers within a 100-mile radius or grow your own food wherever possible. This concept has been consistently promoted by the United Nations. Olivier De Schutter, UN Special Reporter states, "We won't solve hunger and stop climate change with industrial farming on large plantations ... The solution lies in supporting small-scale farmers."[316]

In collaboration with 60 world governments and 400 specialists, the World Bank, the United Nations and the World Health Organization found that "not only would industrial food production not be able to feed the world in the long term, but the practices being employed are actually increasing hunger, exhausting resources and exacerbating climate change."[317] And in a 2010 report from the Human Rights Council, they recommended "supporting decentralized participatory research [and investing in] agricultural research ... public goods rather than private goods ... forms of social organization [and] creating a macro-economic enabling environment."[318] However, this goes against the values of today's consumer culture. It would go against the ideas of globalisation, stockpiling wealth, and resource control.

As a by-product of mass profit-led productions, 40% of food goes uneaten in America[319]. Through empowering our communities and allowing them to become self-sufficient, they can become far more resourceful. They can dictate their own needs and set examples for a sustainable future. They can reduce packaging and air-miles, focus on nutritional food and embrace renewable resources. They can help and support one another. They can become a community.

# Trial and Error

I believe that our consumer system is so all-encompassing that we are yet to understand the full consequences. Therefore, if we were to explore a new system it would likely be compromised by our current modes of thinking. We would unavoidably carry with us some residue of previous ideologies. This is one of the many reasons that I'd advocate not only exploring completely new systems but ones that continue to evolve as we gradually remove the stubborn stains of previous times.

If we take the example of someone who was raised in a violent household; if they move into a house with people who don't hit each other but still aggressively shout at each other, then the individual may incorrectly view it as a compassionate environment. They may have identified physical violence as wrong and changeable, but due to their limited perspective they might misidentify verbal violence as expected and healthy. If they then work for a negative corporation, where people also shout at each other or undermine each other, their misconceptions of possibilities may solidify.

In short, we haven't tried every possible system, therefore we cannot say the current system is our best option. We also cannot fully understand what the best possible option would be unless we experiment.

In these chaotic times, we need method, we need scientific approaches. And we need to remain humble to accept that what we thought was the right alternative may well be proved to be wrong. And rather than hiding from this possibility we should continue to be critical. We can't fall for the all-too-tempting trap of becoming married to one's ideas. An optimal system will have to be incredibly adaptable. It needs to be prepared to redefine that which we assume to be a given. By acknowledging the latest evidence and embracing change we could be progressing at lightning speed rather than a meek, half-hearted amendment here or there.

We are currently 'fine tuning' a legacy system as though it is almost perfect. And as a result we are letting huge leaps pass us by every day.

Even within very confined areas, we can see that those who have embraced the latest scientific findings and were openminded enough to experiment have been able to achieve great things:

· In 2001 Portugal took the radical decision to decriminalize drugs, and instead implement more treatment-orientated deterrents. Despite the international backlash, drug use has consistently fallen and they have seen a huge decrease in HIV and overdose deaths[320]. In fact, Portugal has 3 overdose deaths per million citizens, whereas the average for the EU is 17[321].

· Up to the late 1970s Iceland was largely relying on imported fossil fuels for its energy supplies. However, with rising costs, Iceland were in many ways forced to innovate. What began as small experiments on farms and various incentive programs led to wide-scale solutions. Today almost 100% of Iceland's consumed energy comes from their own renewables: geothermal and hydropower[322]. They are now leaders in sustainability and far less reliant on imports and external markets.

· In 2005 Lloyd Pendleton, director of Utah's Homeless Task Force, launched an innovative strategy to combat out-of-control levels of homelessness: he gave them homes. Having a safe place to call home became a right. He started with around 20 people to test the waters and gradually expanded. While other states had rising numbers of homelessness, Utah saw a 74% decline[323]. And perhaps most surprisingly, it actually cost the government far less. While a homeless person can cost the state over 30,000 dollars in social services, medical treatments, police calls, court hearings etc, the price of modest housing and counselling is less than a third of that amount[324]. Currently Utah is on track to completely eliminate homelessness and all the while save money.

· Denmark is already the leader with regards to efficient, sustainable, and organic agriculture; however, it only continues to ramp things up and set new standards. The Danish government recently announced an impressive 67-point plan of attack to double their organic production by 2020[325]. To increase consumer awareness they inform the public about sustainable organic farming as well as enforcing mandatory labelling of genetically engineered foods[326]. Due to their pioneering approach to food production, Denmark is able to provide canteens, hospitals and nurseries with an abundance of healthy organic meals every day[327].

· For the past 40 years Finland has experimented with huge educational reforms; such as less exams, less homework, smaller class sizes, less formality, more breaks, shorter days and more qualified teachers with a tighter screening process. Through an open-minded and scientific attitude, Finland went from average performances to consistently coming first in the international education system's rankings[328].

· Despite the seemingly high risk, Norway decided to experiment with a less punitive and more rehabilitative prison system. The prisoners are given greater freedom, they can spend more time outside, they have access to workshops and libraries and they are treated with respect. Contrary to what international justice systems had previously assumed and preached, Norway's decision was a resounding success. Not only does Norway have incredibly low rates of crime, it also has one of the lowest figures in the world for returning offenders, at just 20%[329]. By contrast, in the U.S, over 75% of prisoners are re-arrested within just five years[330]. While Norway may appear to have taken a leap of faith, they are purely following the latest evidence which shows that strict incarceration actually increases re-offence and that rehabilitation can indeed rehabilitate[331].

Sadly, even with these now tried-and-tested reforms, other countries are stuck in old and often harmful ways. If we learn that certain jobs or lifestyles are affecting our mental and physical health, if we learn that certain practices are unsustainable, and if we learn that there is a better way in any given sector, we should be able to adapt accordingly. We should be humble enough to accept our mistakes and update our systems as there is a shameful amount of room for improvement.

I am not suggesting we blindly follow science. But we should have systems that are prepared to change. We could have much more experimentation, more scientific rigour, and a system whereby successes can be effectively relayed to the general public which could automatically trigger a vote for reform.

There could be many advantages within our hypothetical models, and a Free System could evolve and expand in numerous ways. However, is it realistic? What are the biggest concerns or obstacles?

# CHAPTER 10

# CONCERNS & SUCCESSES

Why and why not?

To explore some potential concerns with a Free System, let's take a look at some questions that might come up.

Is this left-wing, centre or right-wing?
This is something new. It is an active democracy within a fluid framework. We can decouple policies from political parties. Some challenges may require a solution from one school of thought, others may require one from outside of current frameworks.

We can move away from backroom deals within a one-size-fits-all rigid system towards a modular set of evolving sectors. A Free System can move away from the restrictive two-party popularity contest where what's best for the party is not inherently best for the people. The system can evolve to make best use of the latest knowledge. It can also be light on its feet and reverse out of bad decisions. It can accept when it is wrong and it can go boldly towards a brighter future.

Will we stop progressing?
This is not about halting progression, it is about progressing in ways that are

sustainable and safe with regards to our mental and physical health.

In today's market the idea of regulations has been misidentified as holding humanity back rather than protecting humanity. As corporations can now buy reform and fund political parties, they can continue to deregulate. Therefore they can further increase profits, and further shape the system to fit their needs.

If a new development can be proven to increase corporate profits it can be unchallenged, green-lit and hastily rolled out. A simple example of this is plastic packaging; which was implemented worldwide before we knew how to manage it responsibly. In fact, many countries still have zero recycling and yet the majority of their products are covered in plastic. This means that various bags, containers and other items can be found all around our cities, in our soil and in our oceans. A specific example would be in Bali, Indonesia where locals have to sieve soil for days before they can plant in their own gardens due to plastic waste.

Despite our valiant efforts to sieve the plastic from our lives it is deeply engrained. A recent article published in *Science Reports* showed that of the 16 brands of sea salt analysed, scientists discovered plastic in all but one of them[332]. Another global study revealed that tap water also contains plastic, with over 80% of the samples contaminated[333]. And once something is in your tap water, this also means that it is likely in your clothes, your skin and your diet.

And perhaps it's no surprise that we've arrived at this point as nearly every unit of plastic ever made still exists in some way, shape or form and we only recover 5% of it[334]. In fact, enough plastic is thrown away each year to circle the Earth four times and we continue to increase our output[335]. Over the last ten years we have produced more plastic than the previous 100 years combined[336].

The technological breakthrough of plastic packaging was short-sightedly implemented for its potential economic benefits well before the long-term impact was fully understood. The planet and the people are the ones who pay the real price for short-sightedness fuelled by money.

In many ways the challenges that we face with regards to plastic epitomise the capitalist mentality of prioritising profit over all else. However, we could be progressing in a new direction with sustainable and healthy limits.

Isn't life supposed to have winners and losers?
It is all too easy to imagine capitalism as a real-life game of Monopoly, where if you play the game well you will win, and if you can't keep up then you'll lose. This idea is especially appealing to the current winners.

Monopoly works as a game as everyone starts in the same position, with the same resources, and at the same time. In 'real-world Monopoly' this is not the case. And not everyone is getting $200 for passing go nor does everyone have the chance to receive a Get Out Of Jail Free card. The board game is also sustainable as playing the game doesn't destroy natural resources nor impact those around you. In the board game once people can no longer pay, the board is wiped clean and you can choose to play again or play something else. In the real-world scenario, power grows and grows and there is no reset button.

Will I have to give up my luxury items?
No. A Free System is not a dictatorship. You will not need to hand over all luxury items nor move house. However, there will be a rational limit to the amount of land that you can use, to ensure a healthy and sustainable food supply and equal opportunity for others. This would be determined by the unbiased Earth Score upon which the public could vote.

With no money, how will we encourage innovators?
While a Free System could work towards equal opportunity, that doesn't mean it has to create equal outcome. Some people may choose to live a more relaxed and social life, others may want to focus a lot of time and energy on development of themselves or a project. To facilitate this we could provide resource grants. Where those who choose to work more and explore certain ideas could be given more time and more resources to achieve certain goals.

We could remove the systemic influence of 'luck' and replace it with a pioneer-rewarding system of merit.

Equal opportunity is fundamental for a successful society, but too often equal outcome is thrown into the same pot. One of the biggest recurring issues with capitalism is that those who often benefit from an unequal opportunity can shape the system and therefore their own outcome.

I feel that with the right system we can curb greed and isolated power, and at the same time create equal opportunities without repressing individual outcome. Resource grants could go to the most well-thought-out plan and we could make more democratic and community-focused decisions. Perhaps you could pitch ideas to an online innovation forum and the public could vote accordingly.


But aren't people just greedy?

Corporations can create and target our insecurities. They can use our vulnerabilities to fuel purchases. The results are devastating in many ways. First of all, they are highly effective as their strategies can target our subconscious mind. Secondly, and perhaps more importantly, due to their often covert methods, even though we have been manipulated, it can be misidentified as simple human nature - unforced with no exploitation.

These covert tactics were in many ways shaped by Ernest Dichter, a pioneering psychologist and marketing expert. In the 1940s, Dichter founded the Institute for Motivational Research, where he began to deconstruct and analyse why people purchase an item. If individuals chose to keep their money instead, he sought to isolate and remove the barriers. He used his psychoanalyst approach–through studies, indirect observations and focus groups–to uncover the subconscious drivers behind consuming.

In *The Century of the Self* [337], Adam Curtis explores one of Dichter's breakthrough discoveries made during a focus group for the Betty Crocker Cake Mix. Pre-prepared convenience food was somewhat of a novelty in the mid-1900s and there was resistance to purchasing these new items. During Dichter's observations, he concluded that there was an underlying guilt due to the convenience of these simplified products[338]. Family cooking traditions were being subconsciously challenged. To remove this barrier to profit, Dichter suggested giving the consumer a greater sense of participation. He told Betty Crocker to add new labelling on the packaging, instructing the consumer to add an egg. They did, and sales soared. The subconscious drivers are so powerful that even a subtle tweak can have a huge impact on the consumer's decision.

Dichter's success redefined the industry. Psychoanalysts became a staple for corporations and political parties. Rather than the simple case of selling an item or implementing reform, we began to enter the realm of selling more ideas, concepts, traditions and narratives. Those out to gain control and profit could delve deeper and efficiently exploit subconscious drivers. This could be used to promote or hinder decisions, and even to create tension between groups. A new, powerful tool had been unleashed and was available to those who could afford it.

Therefore, the question becomes a lot more complicated. Are people inherently greedy? Do they naturally want to fill their time consuming? Or, are they being expertly manipulated? Is it human nature or the consequences of an environment in which corporations need to harvest money? The answer may be somewhere in between, but it is far too easy to forget that our decisions are being guided in many ways. We forget that the packaging, the terminology and the ingredients may have been shaped with the help of psychoanalysts and marketing experts with a growing set of data. There is no clear distinction between the authentic and the manipulated. Betty Crocker 'herself' was a fictional creation of the Washburn-Crosby Company.

What is truth? And what is a useful narrative? We have to first acknowledge we are losing power before we regain control.

Removing money from our system will not completely remove greed or any other negative traits. However, by creating a totally new system, one that re-invents our ideas of ownership, promotes strong contribution communities and is designed to serve us as a collective, then we could see a reduction of greed. Whilst we cannot blame all of humanity's shortcomings on the 'system', we should continue to seek systemic improvements. Our hypothetical system is not perfect, but we are far from competing with perfection.

Isn't full equality impossible?
A Free System promotes rational equal opportunity, not to be confused with an absolute equal society. Therefore, if we have 100 female doctors we wouldn't need to ensure that we equally had 100 male doctors, as this can enter the realm of a dictatorship or social engineering. A Free System seeks a sustainable and fair equality where we provide people equal opportunities of logical, rational and reasonable things, such as health and education. Our push for equality is about treating others as you'd like to be treated; this means providing everybody with the same opportunities you'd like for yourself and your family.

Why can't we just opt out and live in small isolated communities?
Larger systems alongside locally run communities are crucial for our own protection. If we are more integrated we can support others in times of difficulty such as crop failures, natural disasters, climate change and exploitation. Combating these kinds of issues requires a larger framework.

We are used to battling with the 'other'. An authentic solution-focused system would have to move beyond this limiting mentality towards unity. We are currently facing extraordinary social, physical and environmental challenges that affect us all, but we are fragmented into self-serving states that cannot prioritise these issues.

Isn't a Free System a little extreme?

"Remember: those who called for the abolition of slavery, for suffrage for women, and for same-sex marriage were also once branded lunatics."
-Rutger Bregman

Terms such as extremism are often used to negatively label those who fight for positive change. Try not to think of the solution as extreme, but rather the scale of our problems as vast. Slow and gradual progress will not suffice for many of our current challenges. Gradual progression also implies a gross lack of consideration for those currently suffering. For a healthy and abundant future on this planet, we need extreme change.

We often use the word extreme to make our current practices seem more stable and more rational. An example of this could be a vegetarian having a conversation with a vegan about diets. When the vegan states that he or she doesn't eat cheese, the vegetarian may respond with, "I'm not that extreme!" Not only does the term extreme help to justify our current practices, it can also belittle the actions of others, which to them could be an attempt to do the right thing by making a positive sustainable change to help others. A better response could be to support the 'other', ask questions and try to understand their actions and what they are trying to achieve before labelling it as 'extreme'.

"Most misunderstandings in the world could be avoided if people would simply take the time to ask, 'What else could this mean?'"
-Shannon L. Alder

Can't we just improve the current system?
Too frequently do we attempt to 'solve' recurring symptoms rather than the root causes. When an unsustainable and immoral system crashed in 2008, we looked at the symptom–a lack of money–and we tried to treat it by giving it more money. We put a small temporary band-aid on a deeply infected wound. It was the equivalent of, in the famous words of Lewis Mumford, "loosening your belt to cure obesity."[339] Rather than maintaining an unsustainable system that benefits a few, can't we dare to create a far better one? I, like many others, have grown tired of the half-hearted, incremental changes in modern politics and its played-out cycles as the pendulum swings from slightly better to slightly worse.

"Things remain the same because it is impossible to change very much without changing most of everything."
-Ted Sizer


Isn't a national revolution impossible?

No. And in fact, there is a recent example.

In 2009, during what is now known as a 'pots and pans revolution', the people of Iceland grouped together, protested peacefully and created a new government. The people of the revolution elected 25 citizens who didn't represent a former political party, but who were endorsed by the people. They then created their own constitution on the internet, where people were allowed to monitor and contribute. They successfully and peacefully regained control.

This revolution was a direct response to an increasing country debt. Rather than conceding to the traditional 'solution' of a bank bailout, they nationalized Icelandic banks and arrested the bankers. The public refused to pay the debt that was ultimately created by private banks. They refused to fund and continue an unsustainable, unethical and unhealthy practice. However, in America and across Europe, profit-led deceit by the world's banks merited trillions in bailouts and drastic austerity measures for the people.


But aren't things already getting better? Can't we just wait?

To answer this question, let's look at the current water crisis in California.

California has become one of the most manipulated landscapes in the world. Having depleted numerous water sources, wealthy landowners are now mining for water that has taken thousands of years to accumulate. We now have a situation where both local wells and ancient reserves are completely dry, and vast areas are becoming desertified. Meanwhile, those responsible for this crisis are reporting record profits.

One of the key players in this 'game' is Stewart Resnick, president of The

Wonderful Company and Paramount Farms International. He is the owner of vast areas of land and gigantic reserves of water. His minimum wage employees, however, can't even drink their own tap water; and they are not alone, with over 1 million Californian residents currently without access to clean water[340].

Through the accumulation of privatised wealth, Resnick was able to create a monopoly of land and water, circumventing environmental reviews and creating giant underground water banks. The water either goes to his own companies or is sold back to the people with huge profits.

Groundwater is currently unregulated to the extent that as long as you 'own' the land you can claim 'ownership' to any water beneath it. Even if it means that you are taking water from beneath your neighbour's land, which could be part of the same undivided reserve. If you have the money to build a bigger 'straw' and create vast water banks, you can drain the water wells of entire communities. The rate of private water mining is so rapid that the land is constantly sinking, sometimes up to 2ft. per year[341].

On a global scale, increasing amounts of water from numerous countries is being traded and finding its way into the banks of the wealthiest private companies. Water, as with many naturally occurring resources, is quickly becoming a privatised commodity. We can now find water investors, owners, traders and brokers.

With the case in California, new sustainable groundwater regulations are estimated to not be in full effect for at least another 20 years[342]. The slow 'regulations' may actually exacerbate the problem, as now the landowners are racing to the bottom of 'their' water reserves to ensure the best return on investment. As Environmental Attorney Doug Obegi states, "There is certainly a fear that we are closing the barn doors after the horses have left the farm."[343] What use are sustainable water regulations in over 20 years' time when you have no water left or it has all become privatised?

Human beings may always have the natural capability of cruelty and greed, but can't we greatly improve things by imposing immediate restrictions backed by science? Only a few people would object to this, the 'owners' such as Resnick and the law-making alliances that the private 'owners' continue to fund.


## Successes

Despite the often-daunting goal of systemic change, we can draw inspiration from those who are already part of a solution:

· In 2015, Seattle-based CEO Dan Price announced that he would slash his own ~$1 million salary to $70,000 and raise the minimum wage for all of his employees to match his own[344].

· In the face of the seemingly impossible task of removing plastic from our oceans, college friends Andrew Cooper and Alex Schulze rose to the challenge and started the 4 Ocean company. Together, with the help of volunteers from all around the world, they have removed nearly a quarter of a million pounds of plastic and they continue to expand on the operation[*].

· PlasticPurgery.com, a volunteer-run start-up, have set out to make it as easy as possible to source alternatives to limited-use and single-use plastics, thus empowering the public to prevent plastic pollution from the source.

· An urban ecovillage project completed feasibility tests for five sites in Australia in 2016[345]. Ben O'Callaghan, director of the movement, aims to create sustainable, community-focused, urban housing settlements. Interestingly, O'Callaghan uses Dunbar's Number, as the sites will scale up to a maximum of 150, enabling the residents to foster strong and genuine relationships within their community.

· In 2017, volunteers in India planted 66 million trees in just 12 hours[346].

---

[*] Find out more at 4ocean.com
164

There is also an array of new grassroots political parties forming that come from outside of the current system and are prepared to explore something new. An interesting example is The Initiative Party in Sweden. The party have declared a list of clear values, as well as a list of crises the party must address: the mental health crisis, the environmental crisis and the crisis of a diminishing democracy.

Like a Free System they aim to be transparent about their intentions and tackle controversial challenges that are seemingly ignored within our current systems. The Initiative's ideas stem from the school of thought of metamodernism where one combines critique of postmodernism with a shared responsibility for a brighter future[347]. The party's vision is said to be one which is "happy, healthy, sustainable and co-created."[348] They follow a similar philosophy and practice to The Alternative Party from Denmark, which has been said to represent "the revolution of culture capital against economic capital."[349] Both parties move away from rigid and ready-made political programs towards a list of morals and ongoing solution-focused, democratic workshops. Both parties seek to reduce the influence of wealth and isolated power.

Another source of inspiration are the many movements around the world that focus on alternatives to our ancient monetary system:

The Venus Project

The Venus Project promotes a moneyless, resource-based economy. Founder Jacque Fresco, produced articles, books and films to promote a more sustainable way of life, and his team are moving towards building a test city to explore, develop and further promote his ideas. Their cities would move away from a focus on profits to a focus on the quality of life.

Million Mask March

The Million Mask March is an annual event that takes place every year on the 5th of November in cities across the world, with some of the largest events taking place in Washington and London. Although the specific causes behind the march vary, the uniting goal is raising awareness to current injustices as well as calling for a brand-new political system.

## Free World Charter

The Free World Charter is an online list of ten principles that promote a world without money and a new system "based on fairness, common sense and survival."[350] Everyday increasing numbers from across the world are signing the Free World Charter and supporting a world without money.

## A Featherway

A Featherway is a new online platform where you can acquire what you need through the sharing, gifting and trading of experiences, help, skills and items. The free and easy-to-use website[*] allows you to create or join a mini-economy in your area without the need of money. For example, you could exchange bike repair for some food, or guitar lessons for gardening. You could use it every day or just a few times a month. It allows you to become less reliant on money as well as fostering a stronger and more resilient community. Similar platforms include Freeworlder, Freecycle, Kindista, Karmatribe and Streetbank.

## Time Banking

Time-based currencies in industrialized Western societies go back as far as the 19th century. In 1832 Robert Owen founded the National Equitable Labour Exchange whereby labour was considered as wealth, with hours becoming the principle unit of currency. Robert Owen was a true pioneer of moneyless economies despite conflicts with large corporations and severe repression from the government. In the 90s the movement expanded, led by Edgar S. Chan and Martin Simon. Today there are thousands of active time banks across 26 countries and the movement continues to grow, facilitated in part by free and easy-to-use software[*].

---

[*] Afeatherway.com
[*] Such as Community Weaver3, Community Forge, and Time and Talents.

The Open Economy
Author and social activist Colin R. Turner frequently advocates for a world without money. In his book *Into the Open Economy*, he explores the limitations of capitalism as well as promoting a new system without money, trade and governance[351].

Ubuntu Contributionism
This movement was founded by Michael Tellinger and calls for a world without money. His philosophy carries a five-point mantra, "No money, no barter, no trade, no value attached, everyone contributes their skills for the greater benefit of all in the community."[352] Ubuntu Parties have participated in national elections, and are gaining momentum all around the world. They are currently focusing on their One Small Town movement, where they aim to create a series of contribution communities through a cooperative workforce. Recently they announced the first mayor to adopt the system: Mayor Ron Higgins of North Frontenac, Ontario, Canada, thus showing that contribution economies within the Western world are indeed greater than fiction.

The Free Collective
In addition to the above, other movements that promote moneyless ideals include Woofing, Zeitgeist, Moneyless Society, Money Free Party, Permaculture, New Earth Nation and Community Planet.

When a large tree falls it can make a tremendous noise that shakes the ground. But a new tree growing is silent and can, for some time, go completely unnoticed. While we may see and hear bad news, there is plenty to feel optimistic about rising up all around us; and we can be part of that, if we partake in solutions.

# Automated Change

In ancient Rome certain leaders freely offered food and entertainment to the public. This was done to combat, amongst other things, huge rates of unemployment. In modern times, unemployment rates are predicted to rise due to the rapid development of automation technology. Could this necessitate the transition to free resources and, perhaps, a moneyless economy?

About 40 years ago, home computers were introduced. Today, we carry them in our pockets. The advancements in technology seem to constantly double every 18 months, often referred to as Moore's law[*].

The first computers were designed by hand; now the computers themselves assist us. Not only the design software, or the sharing of knowledge, but also manufacturing and transport. This technology doesn't ask for holidays, sick leave, a pay rise or even a lunch break. It will happily work around the clock, day and night.

Accordingly, Oxford University economists Doctors Carl Frey and Michael Osborne state that 40% of jobs may be lost to automation by 2050[353]. A recent University of Toronto article revealed that, when looking at the Canadian job market, there are "7.5 million jobs that could be at risk of automation."[354] And according to Elon Musk, "[Eventually] the robots will be able to do everything."[355]

Certain sectors will be automated before others, which could lead to social frictions and class struggles. In a recent Business Insider report it was revealed that, "while many metropolitan cities will lose more than 60% of their jobs, people in higher-paying careers are less likely to be impacted."[356] In order to protect against mass poverty and social unrest, numerous countries around the world–including the Netherlands, Italy, Finland, Canada, Kenya and the UK–are trialling a universal basic income (UBI).

The largest UBI experiment in history was in Manitoba, Canada, where

---

[*] Moore's Law refers to an observation by Gordon Moore, where by the number of transistors on integrated circuits seemed to double every 18 months.

168

for five years monthly cheques were delivered to those below the poverty line. Poverty in the area vanished overnight. There was always food on the table, giving people stability and assurance. It allowed people to be more strategic and less reactive. One resident, for example, signed up for training and got a part-time job which eventually led to a full-time career[357]. In fact, the experiment was a resounding success in many ways. It resulted in more sustainable birth rates and improved school performance[358]. It also resulted in the reduction of hospitalisations, mental health problems and domestic violence[359]. So what happened to the Manitoba experiment?

It was closed down in 1979 by the Conservative government of Sterling Lyon and the results were not released[360].

When you consider the increase in automation, subsequent rising rates of unemployment and an uncontrollable runaway debt crisis, then perhaps a mass re-evaluation of money is inevitable.

"We are on the verge of a cashless society, so my question to you is, what do you want a cashless society to look like?"
-David Birch

Could UBIs be the final catalyst to redesigning our concepts of ownership, resource control, and stockpiling wealth? Could it facilitate a more open mind towards a completely money-free society? Could it evolve into some form of contribution card?

In the following chapters we will shift away from hypothetical theories. We will discuss how all of us can help to make a better world–starting today. This will include ambitious action items as well as simple daily tricks and tips that move towards a logical, healthy and sustainable future.

How do we transform utopian concepts into actionable tasks with visible results?

# PART III

# HOW CAN WE HELP TODAY?

A step-by-step plan of attack

CHAPTER 11

# ACTION ITEMS

How can I help today?

## Step 1: Acknowledgement

**B**efore real change happens, we must first fully accept that there are indeed huge flaws and injustices within our current system. This is not to be confused with being ungrateful nor having a false sense of entitlement; this is the acceptance that many are, and many will be, unnecessarily suffering if we continue with business as usual.

We can acknowledge there is an increasing gap between rich and poor, increasing mental health issues, increasing division, increasing environmental damage and increasing global debt. We can acknowledge that huge swaths of third-world countries are carrying the true weight of Western abundance. We can rethink our addictions and comforts and be prepared to pull back the curtains and see the consequences of profit and luxury.

We can acknowledge two fundamental truths: one, that there is indeed a problem, and two, that we can do something about it. This is beyond the regressive sentiment of making things great 'again'. We can learn from our past and present to improve our futures. The problems of the current system are there for all to see. The excuse of ignorance is no longer justifiable.

"If we can really understand the problem, the answer will come out of it, because the answer is not separate from the problem."
-Jiddu Krishnamurti

Before we start the next steps, please remember I do not condone violence. A revolution can be passionate yet peaceful. I don't want people to suffer nor do I want the current system to explode. I want to help people. I want to propose a new system as well as tangible action items so that solutions don't have to come from resentment, fear or hatred.

In times of revolution I don't want a reactive, unconsidered system where the same issues arise, in a new envelope, with the same mind-set that created the root of our problems. I would like us to reach our full potential by exploring new avenues for effective change.

## Step 2: Spread the Message

"You are personally responsible for becoming more ethical than the society that you grew up in."
-Eliezer Yudkowsky

To rid the world of corruption, exploitation and harmful practices is an incredibly ambitious quest and it cannot happen without your active engagement. Please help to spread awareness of both the challenges and potential solutions. This is vital during our highly conservative time, with deeply entrenched narratives and ancient ideologies. Proactive individuals are crucial for grassroots movements such as this. More and more people are waking up and seeing the truth. We can accelerate this.

"Our lives begin to end the day we become silent about things that matter."
-Martin Luther King Jr.

# Step 3: Question

One of our biggest weaknesses is that we have stopped asking questions, to the extent where those who question things are automatically viewed as conspiracy theorists, selfish, unpatriotic or just plain crazy. Ironically, through questioning your practices you are actually being very scientific, you are selflessly trying to do the right thing, you are protecting those around you and you are highly engaged. This is not about insulting or shaming anyone; it is about understanding what is going on in order to learn how we can help.

Questioning is one of the most important things we can do to incite change, as without doing so we are easily exploited and harmful acts can remain hidden. We cannot afford to become idle consumers when the system's focus is often capital and not necessarily our well-being or future. We have started to stop asking basic questions such as: what is this? How was it made? Where does it come from? Is it sustainable and healthy? Does it help us?

To give a simple example let's question a single item. Let's look at a McDonald's Big Mac. To start things off, let's begin with a seemingly simple question:

What is it?
This is a question most people will likely already know the answer to. It is of course a burger, a fast food product from a well-known multinational company. But what actually is it?

It's 540 calories, 45 grams of carbohydrates, 9 grams of sugar, and so on. You could also say that it's 43% of our recommended sodium, 45% of our recommended fat, and 50% of our recommended trans-fatty acid. We may have had to do a bit of research, but we can find out what we are putting into our bodies. We might determine that a Big Mac is not really very good for you, but one every now and then isn't going to kill you.

But even after these preliminary questions, we still don't really know what it is. How many ingredients does it have? And what are they?

Just by looking at a Big Mac on the menu board we might guess seven ingredients:

· Bread
· Beef
· Cheese
· Lettuce
· Onions
· Pickles
· Sauce

But what if we started to look at the raw components? Let's hypothesise that the sauce is made from three ingredients. And you may know that bread is traditionally made from flour, water and yeast, plus we can see sesame seeds on top of the bun. So at first glance we said seven ingredients, but if we stop and think about it, and guess a little, it could be twelve:

· Flour
· Water
· Yeast
· Sesame seeds
· Beef
· Cheese
· Lettuce
· Onions
· Pickles
· Unknown sauce component 1, 2, and 3

174

In fact, you may be surprised to hear that there are actually over 70 ingredients, and there may well be a great deal more[361].

Here is a full breakdown starting with the heart of the item, the beef:

· Beef
· Salt
· Pepper

Let's skip over the fact that we don't know what part of the cow was used nor which antibiotics, growth hormones and other chemicals have been injected and instead continue with the generous salad:

· Onions
· Lettuce

Plus those famous pickles which are actually:

· Cucumbers
· Water
· Distilled Vinegar
· Salt
· Calcium Chloride
· Alum
· Extractives of Turmeric
· Potassium Sorbate
· Natural Flavours
· And Polysorbate 80

The 'cheese' is known as Pasteurised Processed American Cheese and it contains:

· Milk

- Cream
- Water
- Sodium Citrate
- Cheese Cultures
- Salt
- Colour Added
- Sorbic Acid
- Citric Acid
- Lactic Acid
- Acetic Acid
- Enzymes
- And Soy Lecithin

It's probably safe to say at this point that there are quite a few ingredients the majority of people wouldn't know and certainly wouldn't have on their shopping lists or in their kitchen cupboards.

In addition to this, some items are not an identifiable ingredient such as "Natural Flavours", which is disconcertingly pluralised. We also have the 'ingredient' "Colour Added", which is also highly ambiguous.

Next up we have the infamous Big Mac sauce:

- Soybean Oil
- Diced Pickles
- High Fructose Corn Syrup
- Sugar
- Vinegar
- Salt
- Calcium Chloride
- Xanthan Gum
- Potassium Sorbate
- Spice Extractives
- Polysorbate 80

- Distilled Vinegar
- Water
- Egg Yolks
- Onion Powder
- Spices
- Corn Syrup
- Propylene Glycol Alginate
- Sodium Benzoate
- Mustard Bran
- Garlic Powder
- Hydrolyzed Corn
- Soy
- Wheat
- Caramel Colour
- Extractives of Paprika
- Soy Lecithin
- Turmeric (Colour)
- And Calcium Disodium EDTA

It's worth noting that the "Diced Pickles" in the sauce would be made from multiple ingredients and there is yet more ambiguity with components such as "Caramel Colour", "Spice Extractives", and "Spices".

Finally let's take a look at the simple, age-old staple, bread:

- Riboflavin
- Enriched Unbleached Flour
- Wheat Flour
- Niacin
- Malted Barley Flour
- Reduced Iron
- Thiamin Mononitrate
- Folic Acid

- Water
- Yeast
- Soybean Oil
- Salt
- Wheat Gluten
- Sesame Seeds
- Calcium Sulfate
- Ammonium Sulfate
- High Fructose Corn Syrup
- And Calcium Propionate

The bread also comes with an ingredients disclaimer of "May Contain One or More Dough Conditioners (Sodium Stearoyl Lactylate, DATEM, Ascorbic Acid, Mono and Diglycerides, Monocalcium Phosphate, Enzymes, Calcium Peroxide)."

So in fact, with the Big Mac, when we ask 'what is it?' perhaps the simplest and safest answer is 'we don't know'. We don't know what we are putting into our bodies.

I'm sure you could write an entire book just on the ingredients of a Big Mac, so let's just look at one item that appears in both the bread and the sauce, the notorious high fructose corn syrup. There are countless papers, articles and other resources which heavily critique high fructose corn syrup, which I encourage you to read. But for now let's take a look at a single quote:

"Cut the high fructose corn syrup from your life forever. You'll be healthier. Our planet will be healthier. And we'll have a healthier generation of children."

-Mark Hyman, M.D

With all those ingredients there's quite literally an awful lot to digest. It's also worth adding that we don't know the quality of those ingredients and the cooking methods used. It's also worth thinking about the journey and origin of the ingredients. Where do they come from? How are they made and transported? Which companies are involved? Which leads us to the next critical question:

Who made it?
There could be thousands of people all around the world contributing to a Big Mac. Are you happy with their practices and their social and environmental impact?

Let's take a look at one of the companies that we know are definitely involved: McDonald's. At the very least we know they are the company who carry out the final preparations and sell the item. We should, as a customer, be in line with their morals and ethics before we financially support them. So what do we know about McDonald's?

We know about the company's roots, we can see the original co-founders are well documented as receiving a horrendous handshake deal and were reported to be bullied out of the company by businessman and franchiser Ray Kroc[362]. We know the company sells other products too. They also sell salads which might appear like they are genuinely trying to provide a healthy option. However, it was revealed just one of their salads can contain the same number of calories as three McDonald's hamburgers, largely due to their highly calorific dressing[363]. We know they are a giant corporation: in fact, they are the largest franchiser and the largest fast food company in the world[364], with 70 million customers daily[365]–more than the entire population of France. To grow the brand even further they spend nearly $100 million a year on advertising[366]. We can also see that they are involved in extreme-scale tax avoidance, with recent reports by Public Services International revealing how they exploit tax loopholes to avoid paying billions of dollars[367]. We know that McDonald's, with more than 36 thousand locations and a vast array of ingredients, must use up a huge amount of the world's resources[368]. They sell 5 billion burgers a year, which requires an estimated 25 million cows[369]–to put that in perspective, the total human population of Australia, is 24 million. We know the company promotes inequality as a McDonald's employee working overtime for nearly four months straight would earn what the company's CEO does in a single hour[370]. In other words, before lunchtime on January 1st, the CEO will have made an entire year's worth of salary with overtime. Which leads me to my final question:

What does it cost?
The simple answer would be that a Big Mac costs around $5. However, is that the real cost? Does this item just impact your pocket?

In order to keep this brief let's focus on the beef within the Big Mac. Another cost would be the very valuable cost of land. Animal agriculture takes up one third of the Earth's ice-free land area. And as mentioned previously, cow products are an incredibly inefficient return on investment as it takes approximately 2500 gallons of water[371] and 7 pounds of grain[372] to make a single pound of beef. In fact, a meat eater's diet requires 18 times more land than that of a vegan's[373].

What about the environmental costs? How much does this product contribute to greenhouse gases? While many other animals don't create that much methane, cows certainly do. A single cow can produce 250-500 litres of methane per day[374]. Methane is 25-100 times more destructive than $CO2$[375]. Cows also create a lot of manure; in fact, they create 3 times more than humans[376]. Cow manure releases nitrous oxide which has 296 times the global warming effect of $CO2$, and it stays in the atmosphere for 150 years[377]. Cow manure is responsible for two-thirds of all the nitrous oxide pollution in the world[378].

What about the cost to other animals? Cow manure and the fertiliser used to grow their feed ends up in our oceans and creates vast dead zones where no life can survive[379]. In addition to this, 91% of Amazon deforestation is caused by raising livestock[380].

Indeed there are a great number of costs to consider, especially the health costs of highly processed fast food, which is aggressively marketed towards our children. In short, the costs soon add up to more than 4 dollars and 79 cents.

"The general population doesn't know what's happening, and it doesn't even know that it doesn't know."
-Noam Chomsky

We can make well-informed decisions by asking questions such as: What is it? Who made it? And what are the costs? Become engaged, research and share your findings. Protect yourself and those around you. You are merely helping those in your community to make a choice that fits with their own beliefs. Be open about your sources and allow others to critique and contribute. Try to source peer-reviewed studies and look into who is funding the research.

We can all learn together if we are respectful and compassionate. As we question more we will see that our governments and corporations are not asking simple questions on our behalf. Don't blindly trust them as their primary focus is often profit. Question them and don't let scale affect your morals and values.

"In a time of universal deceit, telling the truth is a revolutionary act."
-George Orwell

Questioning and revealing sources and truths becomes increasingly important as we begin to see 'grey areas' around truth and science with terms such as 'alternative facts' and 'true facts'. We have also sadly entered an era of anti-campaigns where 'politicians', rather than discussing policies, seem to focus on spreading misinformation about the opposition through repetitive, false sound-bites; superficial, inaccurate and personal attacks; and social media clickbait.

Scientific study and questioning becomes crucial when we are in the middle of a conflict between inconvenient truths and convenient marketing narratives. Seeking to understand the larger impact is vital as we can easily become independent consumers, unaware or even indifferent to the social and environmental consequences of our actions.

"People want change even when they are resistant to it ... they want a better economy, they want to feel connected, they want social justice, they want to protect the environment. But somehow it is still really hard for them to engage ... because the process forces us to take a really good hard look at our own lives and make some pretty big changes."
-Sash Milne

# Step 4: Vote without Money

Every time you buy something you are keeping that operation going, you are supporting that item and therefore that company's values. You are sustaining them.

People often say, "If I had more money I would make the world a better place." However, these people are often financially supporting the problems. People also say that if they were part of the government they would close down immoral businesses. However, we don't need to ask for permission or wait for the chance to be in power; we can take much needed reform into our own hands.

If we stop funding those that are irresponsible they have to cease operations or dramatically improve. This movement of acknowledgement, questioning, sharing information and then stopping our funding and support for those who work against us, helps us to create communities where we look out for one another.

"Neither a wise nor brave man lies down on the tracks of history for the train of the future to run over him."
-Dwight D. Eisenhower

We have become so disconnected we feel as though we shouldn't be communicating with others. We have become so isolated we may feel anxieties about being openly passionate about something. I urge you to face those fears and fight for a world you believe in. You should feel immense pride as you will be proactively working towards a better world for us all.

Our current systems seem to view physical limitations as negotiable and yet they see man-made economic constraints as non-negotiable. We need to focus on what really matters, what impacts us all. We need to remain open-minded about possible systems and infrastructures as well as implementing and maintaining strict boundaries of power. We have witnessed great change throughout our recent history: equal rights to vote; the civil rights movement; and, more recently, progression with same-sex marriages. However, one could argue that these progressions were greatly simplified as they didn't inherently prevent capital.

What we need now from an environmental perspective requires numerous companies to stop business and others to implement drastic restrictions. These authentic solutions will cause great conflict in our current system, so much so that you may feel as though the needed level of change could never happen. This is an understandable assumption as capitalism gravitates towards the bare minimum change with the firm caveat of continued financial growth. However, we can render much-needed reform, a financially motivated issue. If we choose to no longer fund these companies, we can necessitate change.

## Step 5: Become a Game Changer

"You must be the change that you wish to see in the world."
-Mahatma Gandhi

Create the Alternatives
While some may say that individual change is not sufficient or even that it is a waste of time, I believe that anything we can do to reduce the suffering of others should be done, as this is what we'd expect for ourselves. Being a game

changer is about moving from theory to practice. It is about washing the blood from our hands and inspiring others by positive example. The crises that we face today are perhaps best described as symptoms: symptoms of us. A game changer doesn't search for excuses nor that which removes them from a solution. A game changer takes responsibility for a better future and becomes engaged before 'now' is too late.

You don't have to wait for companies and governments to slowly improve. You can create alternatives. If you are not happy with the number of cars on the road, start riding your bike or start a car-sharing group in your community. If you are not happy with the number of plastic bags being used in your community, write a letter to your local shops and start a petition to ban them in your town, hand out reusable bags and spread awareness. If there are no companies you agree with in your area, start one. If you can't find detailed information on a given company, demand their transparency. We don't have to idly consume and follow the set system. We can set our own paths. We can change the 'game'.

"Where we invest our time in action is how we show the people around us that this is what we actually care the most about."
-Sash Milne

A danger of the current rise of individualism is that we might maintain a passive state through the relentless quest of transient, material possessions. Purchasing becomes the way we express ourselves. Consumer culture can create malnourishing and unsustainable highs that block compassion and prevent action. However, we can transcend beyond the limitations of individualism, narcissism and passiveness to a cohesive and compassionate community: a communicative group who unite and proactively sculpt sustainable environments.

"To improve is to change, to be perfect is to change often."
-Winston Churchill

## Support Other Just Causes

Within capitalism, various groups are pushed to the breaking point at different times. This is made very clear through demonstrations for women's rights, marches in support of same-sex marriages and the recent example of Walmart employees protesting for fair wages. Doctor, teacher and train strikes become part of normal life. Not always, but frequently, a large percentage of those protesting are those personally impacted. An aim of our collaborative movement is to create such unity and strength that should an injustice appear the whole community, even those seemingly 'unaffected' by the repression, will unite and revolt as one.

"None of us are free, if one of us are chained."
-Solomon Burke

## Proactive Syntax and Direct Action

The words we formulate can limit us and build barriers. Some of the sentences we use can appear as though we are being proactive and yet we could be pushing something away, creating an excuse or disguising procrastination.

An example of these speech patterns is, "If only I had more time I could..." While in some cases time may well be a legitimate reason we are in control of how we prioritise it. A statement such as, "If I had more time I would love to learn a foreign language" has neither action nor accountability. A more proactive, helpful and determined sentence would be, "I am now learning a foreign language as I have created the time to read text books during my bus ride commute, I listen to audio lessons at the gym and I have enrolled on an evening course. I will have learned the basics within three months." In contrast, we frequently set measureless and open goals through sentence handles such as, "Someday I'd love to..."

"There are 7 days in a week and 'some day' isn't one of them."

-Benny Lewis

Language is already limiting by its very nature: we are using a narrow frequency of sound waves to convey a chemical reaction. We don't need to create further barriers by applying a restrictive vocabulary with conditional tenses. We can speak in the present tense with honest, direct, and accountable goals. We can replace sarcastic comments with proactive and compassionate, solution-focused action. There is a huge difference between real possibilities and our expected limitations. The words we use, our interpretations and our attitude can prevent us from creating the life we want to live. However, we don't have to live in an unchangeable 'destiny'. We don't have to live in a pessimistic state where either something exists or it would never work. This certainly isn't the case in history. Over and over again, pioneers have explored new systems and structures, and we will continue to do so as long as we believe we can.

"He who says he can and he who says he can't are both usually right."
-Confucius

Confident and opportunistic people believe they can make a real impact, and as a result they stand a fighting chance at doing so. If your interpretation of your surroundings is that history has already been made and you can't make an impact, then this is the reality you will create.

The danger of a pessimistic syntax is that we can create what is known as a self-fulfilling prophecy or the Pygmalion effect. This is where our preconceived expectations have a direct result on our outcomes or lack thereof. Biased interpretations and negative expectations can become cyclical and drive challenges such as cynicism, depression, self-created barriers and fear.

We can remove these limitations. We can study, collaborate and act and speak with direct, proactive and positive intent. We can manifest the world we want to live in through creative direct action.

## New Virtues and Philosophies

"I was brought up surrounded by people who thought only in terms of money. I hated the deadness of it, the narrow vision of life, the blindness to ideals of truth and wisdom."
-Jacob Needleman

By redefining our systems and becoming more engaged, we can create optimum chances to explore new philosophies, goals, and virtues. Perhaps you may be inspired by the philosophy of Stoicism whereby one focuses on ethics and tries to overcome destructive emotions. You may adopt the stoic virtues of self-restraint, justice, courage and wisdom. Or perhaps you may be inspired by the chosen ways of those practicing Buddhism. This could include Right Thought, whereby you seek to eliminate greed, anger and ignorance. Or perhaps Right Speech, which includes words of truth, compassion and help. You may choose to adopt the self-assessment methods of Benjamin Franklin, who gave himself daily scores based on the practice of his own self-set virtues such as temperance, resolution, moderation, justice and humility.

"It is no measure of health to be well adjusted to a profoundly sick society."
-Jiddu Krishnamurti

Through research and greater mindfulness you may create your own hybrid philosophy with your own virtues, intentions and principles. This can enable us to recondition ourselves from an environment that thrives on materialistic goals and superficial interactions.

## New Choices

"We must be willing to get rid of the life we've planned, so as to have the life that is waiting for us."

-Joseph Campbell

As we become authentic, genuine and proactive truth seekers, we will move away from capitalism and consumerism. We will remove the constraints of past barriers and invent a new wealth of opportunities. The alternatives can seem daunting even when they are logical, genuine and deeply considered. However, we must remind ourselves that some of the best things happen when we are outside of our comfort zones. We must remain strong and try to remain grounded in compassion and evidence; evidence so we can reduce the influence of ego and become more sustainable, and compassion so that we can evolve beyond our current frameworks that result in suffering. We can adopt a zero tolerance to harming others. We can unite and focus on what matters, regardless of our personal religious or political alliances, if we can remain grounded in evidence and compassion.

During our limited time on this planet, we can choose to live lives that are in alignment with our virtues and values. We should listen to the pain that we feel when we know that others are suffering and choose to act. We are most human when we care for others.

## Step 6: Explore New Systems

"Action expresses priorities."
-Mahatma Gandhi

In addition to the positive direct action already noted, we can also experiment with systemic change via a small-scale version of our very own Free System. If we are to shift from entrenched systems we need to experiment. Open-minded pioneers who bring their communities together and are prepared to explore new ideas are far more likely to incite positive change than those who accept their fate.

The previous steps of Acknowledgement, Spread the Message, Question, and Vote without Money already incorporate key principles of a Free System. Building upon this, we can explore stronger communities, more authentic connection and even a localised, time-based and money-free economy.

"A rich person is not the one who has the most, but the one who needs the least."
-James J. Lachard

Personal Level
You don't need to wait for anyone else if you wish to transition into a lifestyle that is, at the very least, a little less focused and dependant on money. You could adopt a more minimalist approach to life. You could consume less, reuse, repurpose and recycle more. You could grow and make more of your own items and trade and exchange more within your community. If we are creative we can find many alternatives for things that are becoming monetised, such as socialising, fitness, entertainment and travel. This can be an incredibly empowering exercise no matter how far you choose to take it.

A Featherway
Building upon this personal transition you could create a free account at afeatherway.com that gives you access to a community who is willing to share, gift, and trade experiences, help, skills and items. This can help you acquire more of what you need without having to use money.

Time Banking
To transition into a time-based contribution economy you could join or create a time bank in your area. With this you could start to 'pay' for things with time, and experiment with a new currency within a larger network.

Ubuntu Contributionism
To take things even further and incorporate larger pieces of infrastructure, you could explore the Ubuntu One Small Town Movement. This could allow

you to transition from a complementary currency into a self-sufficient contribution economy. As mentioned previously, this is already in practice in Ontario, Canada.

A Custom Journey

Please remember this is not an all-or-nothing movement. You may take part in just one of the movements, create some of your own or indeed explore all of the above. You could create your own political parties or activist groups based on many of the ideas in this book. You could start a social media page for your area, set up meetings and start working together. You could use balconies and gardens to produce abundance and then freely offer it to your neighbours. As you develop larger networks you can have a greater influence on your environment. The concept of a Free System was developed with the intention of remaining modular and flexible to allow others to make their own revisions and amendments. It could be the basis for a manifesto or just a source of inspiration and resources.

Extra Help

To further assist your journey with money-free economies, you can visit thefreeworldmovement.com where we have complied some helpful resources. There is a section to assist using afeatherway and starting a time bank, and even information to start or support a money-free political party. There is a vast array of resources detailing how to source and make items yourselves, as well as numerous free alternatives for things that have become monetised. There is also a section offering support and advice should you wish to ask corporations to improve their practices.

In addition to the above, myself and the other volunteers will constantly seek and create new ways to help others, all of which will be freely accessible via thefreeworldmovement.com and illuminatepress.com.

You might not be for a full money-less contribution economy but the consequences of experimenting with one on any scale, such as increased connection, communication and a greater sense of community, are incredibly powerful. This movement is about moving towards proactive communal units that we would instinctively seek if we were unimpeded. Revolution is about recapturing power and choice, and by rebuilding strong, self-sufficient sustainable communities we can. We can unite atomised individuals and destroy the myth that we need multinational corporations or that we have to spend most of our days consuming.

We can regain control of our lifestyles, our communities and our health. I strongly believe that we are collectively intelligent enough to not render our home planet uninhabitable for future generations. I believe that we can turn this ship around in time, away from the iceberg of greed and towards something beautiful. We can think about a future that we feel good about and then make it so.

These are simply some humble ideas. I encourage you to unite and engage however you best see fit. In often overwhelming times, being part of solutions and having open discussions with those around us can be incredibly uplifting. What's more, this doesn't have to be a chore; it can be an exciting and fun process. The road to revolution doesn't have to be gloomy or overcast. The journey alone could set us free.

In many ways the problem is not how, with regards to nuances, but our attitudes. We need to act now, give things a go and really try solutions. Change is inevitable, what really matters is when. We are our biggest limitation, but we are also the change that we seek.

# CHAPTER 12

# TRANSITION

How can we escape old ways?

"We are called to be the architects of our future, not its victims."
-Richard Buckminster Fuller

There is a great transformation on the horizon–a revolution of consciousness. A mass disillusionment where the public re-evaluate and begin to seek a lifestyle that is stripped away from material distractions and superficial nonsense. More and more people will start to unplug from corporations and seek more authentic and healthy connections. People will begin to reject consumerism, materialistic values and a corrupt economic system.

If we are still for a moment we can see it rising up, as all around us is an increasing array of unsettling scenes; when we look around a café and see everyone looking into a screen; when we turn on the TV and find the same old repackaged lies, corporate agendas and unaccountable political sound-bites; when we walk down the street and see the majority of stores are selling things that will make us feel worse; when we see people wearing expensive designer clothing to feel in line with corporate messaging, people wearing face masks to reduce the taste of pollution and headphones to reduce the feeling of isolation; when we find ourselves in mundane and superficial cyclical interactions; when we start to notice our mental and physical health deteriorate from an artificial and sedentary lifestyle; and when we see there is much more to life than the daily grind.

Mental[381] and physical[382] health problems are skyrocketing, as is the difference between rich and poor[383], and alongside this the natural ingredients for life are perishing[384]. These symptoms are deeply connected and stem from a fundamental systemic error: the modus operandi on our finite planet is stuck at more profit and more consumption. In a revolution of consciousness the windows slowly become mirrors. We will see that there was only an illusion of freedom and at the same time we are forced to look at ourselves and contemplate the consequences of our own actions.

One by one we will start to investigate alternative ways of life. There will be a gigantic upswing of counter-culture: a mass awakening. We will reduce our consumption of many things: processed food, technology, advertisements, compromised 'news' feeds. We will add self-enforced limits and begin to make, grow, communicate and share more. There will be transformations in many areas, but most importantly in what we value and what we are prepared to stand up for.

Homo sapiens have explored many ages - the Stone Age, the Bronze Age, the Iron Age and, as of late, the Industrial Age, of which we have only tried for a couple hundred years. Before we seemingly dive headfirst into a Digital, Automated or Artificial Age, we are in desperate need of an Age of Reflection.

## The Transition

Our systems of governance could improve in a number of ways. Likewise, they could also stay the same. We could explore ideal scenarios or we could stay on track towards an increasingly unpleasant endpoint. However, I strongly believe that we have a say in this. Even if only on a minute level, we can push or pull it in one direction or another. Although it may seem like a freight train of chaos is hurtling towards us, we are not tied to the tracks. We can abandon the echo of old narratives.

The challenges that we explored thus far impact us all. What's more, they can be conveyed through the universal language of science. However, are we too deeply entrenched, too addicted or too distracted and fractured to notice and unite?

"As the whole world is sliding into the abyss, people are ignoring that fact and fighting with each other."
-Isaac Asimov

Our current challenges require international cooperation yet how can we achieve this if we can't achieve communal cooperation? If we can't even tolerate our own neighbours? If we can't even dare to think big?

What I have tried to promote throughout this book is an awareness and a push towards experimenting with solutions and, even if only purely science fiction, entertaining the idea of a totally new system. Providing we step up and rise to the task of personal transformation, I believe that we will then see increasingly proactive communities all around the world. Those who feel disenfranchised and concerned about the way things are will increasingly unite and explore solutions. More groups will start to implement sustainable, ethical and community-led practices. This non-confrontational transition can progress alongside current systems.

All around the world this has already begun, not just the communities that we have already explored, such as the eco-villages and the Ubuntu Project, but many more, both independent and those affiliated with other international movements. A great example of this is the Transition Network. As with many of the others, they too have a simple set of rational founding principles, such as acting on the latest evidence, implementing democratic systems, respecting planetary limits and acting with compassion. I'd highly recommend adding the Transition Network* to the list of resources to further explore.

---

* transitionnetwork.org

The various community projects are not only able to reverse many negative side-effects of current systems, they also become increasingly less dependent upon them. For example, many communities have been able to become fully self-sufficient with regards to their food supply. Therefore, the community no longer need the income that they spent on food and perhaps may choose to work less hours as a result. They may also choose to spend that surplus revenue on other sustainable resources, perhaps solar panels or equipment shares, which again frees up resources and increases their freedom. This then empowers various communities to peacefully and proactively transition in varying degrees to new ways of living. And these are not marginal experiments; some of these community projects encompass entire towns with many thousands of people. And they are experimenting with an array of pioneering techniques from cryptocurrencies and contribution economies to edible landscapes and community co-ops.

Indeed the idea of self-led tightly-knit communities is not a new one. With regards to duration it could be viewed as Homo sapiens' most tried and tested system. What's more, it is, to some extent, part of the solution that our greatest minds have always advocated for, from Jean-Jacques Rousseau and Mahatma Gandhi to Isaac Asimov and Noam Chomsky.

What I find most promising about community experiments is their ability to explore solutions in working scenarios in different locations. These communities are not in competition with one another and through various online platforms they freely share advice, blueprints and techniques. In these scenarios governments, corporations and even the monetary system begin to lose their potency. While this doesn't solve problems at a national level, every drop into the pool of proactive solution-driven thinking may well prove to be vital.

I could also see numerous scenarios where various communities can act as testing grounds for larger solutions. One of the biggest reasons behind cynical thinking is that while an idea may appear ideal on paper, in practice may well be another story. If we can prove that new ways of life and new systems can work in practice, then we have a great launch pad for national solutions.

I am confident that if we are proactive, if we listen to science and actively experiment then we can solve our current set of crises. In the famous words of Michelangelo, we can critique by creating. We can show that we can improve our physical and mental health, our environmental impact and our sense of democracy, contribution and purpose. And if we can prove that this works across multiple communities, then I believe that this could lead to a people's manifesto. The people could then demand a referendum and we could finally vote for authentic change.

The transition from small-scale co-op explorations to new political manifestos is already in its development stage. The various communities who operate under the umbrella of the Transition Network will often meet at a national level to hone and define their principles and techniques. The Ubuntu Small Town Movement is working with local governments to form coalitions, where the budget for the town is spent on more sustainable infrastructure, therefore further increasing their self-sufficiency. The Ubuntu Movement also works with the local mayors to create a contribution workforce whereby all of the members of the community have free access to community produce and services. Across Canada numerous activist groups united to outline a new system that addresses their major concerns and works for them all. This resulted in the Leap Manifesto, which is now online and gaining mass support*. And the previously mentioned Initiative Party in Sweden started as a small-scale co-op movement.

I believe that part of the reason we are so overdue a revolution is not necessarily down to a lack of alternatives to capitalism, but how different these alternatives are. I feel that most of us have wised up to the idea that any system could function optimally with one decision maker at the top. We have grown tired of the myth that there will be one nice person who always makes great decisions that benefit us all. This has always led to the harsh déjà vu of disappointment; a new envelope but ultimately the same, albeit reworded message.

Perhaps in a time where we were in groups of 150 then a council of wise elders or even a single leader could have made sense, but now we are 7.5

---

* leapmanifesto.org

billion and counting. Now is the time to leave behind the legacy patriarchs. It is time to put the days of witchcraft and speculation behind us, and embrace science for the common good.

Perhaps one day we will abandon the inefficient process of voting for political parties and unaccountable promises. We could put an end to the world's most expensive popularity contest and instead vote directly for policies and systemic improvements—backed by science, grounded in compassion. Rather than trying to win debates, raise election funds, network with influencers, and tarnish opponents, our politicians could ditch divisive distractions and instead focus on solutions. Perhaps our governments will ultimately be viewed more as our HR departments and facilitators than rulers. Perhaps our leading minds would pitch ideas that could be verified and the public could choose via an online up-down voting system. Each solution could be supported by peer-reviewed scientific journals and throughly trialled. Maybe this couldn't work in a system with bias advertising and stockpileable wealth, but in a new contribution framework, without the influence of a monetary system, perhaps it could. Could we move away from solutions for a few, towards sustainable decisions that have been approved by the greatest percentage of people possible within a unified, ever-evolving system of science?

Our current rigid political system, unaffected by new scientific discoveries and a new array of social, environmental and economic problems, is hurting us every day. We can implement better systems not because we know what's best but because we know that we don't know what's best. Our systems, our communities, and indeed we, should attempt what we believe is the right thing to do, but also be aware of our own fallibility. We will make wrong decisions and so we can't be over-precious or protective of our plans. We should embrace the critiques of science and then democratically vote accordingly.

We could build a new flexible free system, with a clear set of principles voted on by the people, and a set of rational scientific boundaries to protect our freedom. On top of that, we can continue to experiment. The people can run their own places of work and have an equal democratic voice. Communities can gradually take back control. Various groups can explore new farming techniques, new educational methods, new lifestyles and so on. Through an open-source platform we can offer it to everyone. Each community could then vote, trial and perhaps implement an upgrade.

We could transition to a Free System. One that is free to evolve. An open-source political framework. A core set of principles and essential infrastructure followed by a set of modular and evolving ideas. One which could breed unity as well as biodiversity.

I think if we do this right, with the right incentives, we could achieve one of the hardest things to balance in human society; we could facilitate both tightly-knit democratic communities and yet still be cognisant and fully aware that we are all in this together, that we can all learn from each other and that ultimately we are all one community.

Therefore, when people ask me how will we transition to a new system, I say at first there will be an individual transition and, after that, perhaps we will transition one small town at a time.

"Corporations would like to control the conditions of our lives, and millions of people are saying not only do we not need you, we can do it better, we are going to create systems that nourish the earth and nourish human beings … that is where the future lies."
-Vandana Shiva

CHAPTER 13

# (R)EVOLUTION

How do you start a successful revolution?

"It is well enough that the people of the nation do not understand our banking and monetary system, for if they did, I believe there would be a revolution before tomorrow morning."

-Henry Ford

In addition to our current transition, I still see value in more traditional forms of revolution. I wouldn't advocate for an aggressive overthrow of the current regime, certainly not without a clear manifesto which the public have voted upon. However, there may be times when we need to resist situations where we are not given the choice of a vote; for example, the privatising of a public service or the destruction of a vital natural resource. To assist with our more immediate revolutions I have listed some tips below.

Public Protests

A protest is one of the most well-known roads to revolution, but it can be difficult to incite much more than awareness. I have listed some tips to help:

## Clarity

Clarity is crucial in making sure that your message is heard and taken seriously. Below are some hypothetical case study examples of clarity through clear goals, action items, slogans and communications.

· Clear Goal: Greater equality.
· Clear First Action Items:

    1. Higher minimum wage through increased taxation of the top 10%.

    2. Zero tolerance to offshore banking.

· Clear Slogan: United Against Inequality.
· Clear and Rational Communications (concise, accurate sound bites):

    1. 8 people on our shared planet have nearly as much wealth as half of the earth's population[385].

    2. 46 million people are currently living as slaves[386].

    3. People are suffering unnecessarily.

    4. We have the resources and knowledge for a respectful and dignified life for all.

    5. Our politicians should be doing a lot more to help.

Clear action items should ultimately lead to a preconceived systemic change which attacks the root cause of the issue.

## Promotion

You can heavily promote your protest before, during and after the event. You can apply for funding, reach out for support, spread the message and explore various strategies. Not only will this further help to spread your message and inspire others, it will also demonstrate that you are serious about change, you are willing to invest and you have a deeply considered strategy.

## Protest Coalitions

Let's suppose that you are part of a women's rights movement. You could collaborate with other groups, ones that are also ultimately pushing for equality through methods such as the Black Lives Matter movement, a same-sex marriage march or an anti-austerity event. You could group together under the united goal of greater equality. Each group is free to have its own action items, but you can support each other and benefit from larger numbers and greater resources. This can help you break past our social media echo chambers where our individual goals and mindsets are echoed back to us within a similar small group of like-minded people, sometimes creating the illusion of wider scale audiences.

Coalitions help us move beyond individualistic goals towards broader actions that benefit us as a whole. Dr Martin Luther King Jr., one of the most influential people in history, didn't restrict his strive towards equal rights and respect to the black population. In his famous *I Have A Dream* speech[387] he speaks of "Jews and Gentiles ... Protestants and Catholics [as well as] black men and white men" being together and united, all treated with respect and awarded the equal rights to live in peace. The more we collaborate, the more we invite change. This helps us to move away from an 'us vs. them' mentality, towards non-violent, respectful and unifying solutions.

"Never doubt that a small group of thoughtful, committed citizens can change the world. Indeed, it is the only thing that ever has."
-Margaret Mead

Engage Policymakers
Be sure to heavily target those who make the decisions that you are trying to influence. Always treat them with respect, offer clear action items and back up your arguments with well-sourced research.

Commit
With many things worth fighting for it may not be easy, but with a clear plan a protest can be very effective. Aim for clear action items–implementable humanist reforms. Refrain from violence and treat others with respect.

Revolutionary Thoughts

A revolution is not limited to systemic change as you can also create a new environment through a psychological shift. For example, you may want to work in an environment where people help each other more. Perhaps at your current workplace there may be negativity or a dog-eat-dog mentality. In this scenario you can be the change and create a new environment by going out of your way to help everyone around you. This will then inspire others and you will have created a new environment without changing location or causing confrontation. You will have manifested a new reality through a proactive and positive mental transition followed by compassionate action. This method can summarised as 'be kind and be first'.

"If you want others to be happy practice compassion. If you want to be happy, practice compassion."
-The Dalai Lama

This technique allows us to simplify the often-daunting task of creating positive change. Much like an addict can find comfort in the smaller and achievable goal of staying clean one day at a time, we can make a positive difference one action at a time. In doing the best you can manage in the present moment you are being the change. Not yesterday, not someday: now. The accumulative effect of this mentality is mighty and highly contagious.

While we may not be able to control the current mist of chaos, we can control how we treat people, how we interact with one another. We can make the conscious decision to stand up, to speak out and to be kind. This technique contrasts with the often counter-productive tactic of fighting fire with fire—which is unfortunately often the outcome for many revolutionary acts.

"In the practice of tolerance, one's enemy is the best teacher."
-The Dalai Lama

Ignorance often leads to fear, as we fear what we don't understand. A risk of fighting fire with fire is pushing that fear towards hatred which is far more difficult to repair. Those who don't understand may at times look for answers, but those who hate may seek protection of their preconceived interpretations. We can evolve far beyond the ineffective, dated and played-out cycle of fighting fire with fire.

"An eye for an eye only ends up making the whole world blind."
-Mahatma Gandhi

We can tackle fear and ignorance with compassion and education. We can tackle hatred and greed with love and contribution. We can transform these words into direct action, beyond likes, shares, memes and retweets. Beyond thoughts and prayers. This means helping others through non-violent positive acts, regardless of their beliefs. If we communicate more, listen more and help more, we will create a better world and be happier as a result.

"When words are both true and kind. They can change the world."
-Gautama Buddha

United Visions
In our hypothetical system we explored the idea of starting with united goals. We can continue to explore this concept at a personal level. If you find yourself in a debate with someone or a group of people, it's very easy to adopt bad habits and gravitate towards a 'me vs. them' stance—a 'two-party' mentality. In these situations it's best to try to create a link between you both, a uniting vision. You can start by finding the things that you have in common. You might both be parents, perhaps you went to same school, or you enjoy the same music. You can then expand your common ground to include your values and goals, even if they are a seemingly reductive and simple three goals: act sustainably, protect people and maintain a just democracy. Often it is not our end goals that differ but the journey, or even

the terminology.

"It's when the conversation stops that the ground becomes fertile for violence."
-Daryl Davis

We will need to practice our communication skills if we are to create unifying systems. Ideally the concepts would come from outside of traditional politics and be as democratic as possible. The Permaculture Movement* could be a great starting point as it is a system/ ideology that many use all around the world to form new systems and frameworks. Although there is great diversity and many have their own way of practicing it, all practitioners are unified under the core tenets of permaculture: care for the earth, care for the people and set practical limits to growth and consumption. The beauty of this is that it has evolved over time and is not owned by any corporation or political party. Our Free System, for example, as it aims to be unifying was sure to also be in line with the tenets of permaculture.

Entry Points
Please don't feel overwhelmed by the task at hand. These movements and revolutionary tactics have multiple access points. Even making incremental lifestyle changes can make a huge difference.

"How far that little candle throws his beams! So shines a good deed in a weary world."
-William Shakespeare

We don't have to personally take on the full responsibility to 'save the world' and start a national revolution. Perhaps you feel particularly passionate about a given area and choose to research solutions and focus on that specifically. If you do choose this route I encourage you to look for others who are also working towards that goal. A free website such as

---
* Permaculture is a system of design principles inspired by natural ecosystems.

meetup.com is a great resource for finding like-minded people and collaborating. Personally I've always been pleasantly surprised to find people on there tackling the same issues as myself, whatever it may be. And they have always been keen to collaborate and offer support. Should your groups expand further, you can use an open-source voting or decision-making platform* to facilitate fast democratic decisions.

The quest for larger change can be incredibly daunting and at times we might feel as though our individual efforts are not enough. To combat this barrier, we can shift our perception of change. Change can be viewed as a cloud, hanging there waiting to happen. We may not decide when it rains or where, but as long as we continue to contribute and inspire others, the clouds will grow and become heavier. Authentic change will become inevitable. It will pour down and wash away even the most entrenched stains.

"The power for creating a better future is contained in the present moment: You create a good future by creating a good present."
-Eckhart Tolle

Right now in particular, the recipe for revolution is especially potent. Not only do we find increasing environmental evidence of system failure, but we also have a middle class whose opportunities and rights are shrinking, and a rapidly growing under-class who cannot afford to put food on the table or own a home. Even the wealthiest members of society are becoming aware of the limitations of transient superficial highs. More and more people are beginning to witness the shortcomings of a system based on if a number goes up or down. Accordingly, the Associated Press revealed that nearly 80% of Americans are dissatisfied or angry with the federal government and a vast majority believe the country is heading in the wrong direction[388]. Systemic change is long overdue.

I encourage you to help however you can, however you best see fit, and have fun doing so. Imagine what we could achieve if we all tried to help, or if at the very least we caused no harm. Imagine if we tried to be of worth rather

---

* Options include Loomio, Doodle, Survey Monkey, Easy Polls and Poll Everywhere.

than stockpile wealth. Or if we tried to contribute rather than compete. What if we committed to not just being the best husbands or wives, mothers or fathers, siblings and friends, but also the best neighbours and the best strangers?

"It's just a ride, and we can change it any time that we want, it's only a choice."

-Bill Hicks

# CHAPTER 14

# TIMING

When should we act?

"Remember at school sitting in history class thinking, 'If I was alive then, I would have...' Well, you're alive now. Whatever you're doing now will be what you would've done."
-Unknown

When can we transition to a system based on evidence and compassion? Are we too entrenched in harmful practices? Do we value money over humanity? I believe that we can incite change at any time and nothing is a more noble cause than ending suffering and helping others. We can become engaged in this issue right now.

"You don't have to be great to get started, but you have to get started to be great."
-Les Brown

We can construct a society with visionary ideas that are, while ambitious, wholly implementable. When the people decide that now is the time, new pioneering systems become reality. If we act with haste and conviction we can see extreme positive change within our lifetimes.

"The climate clock is striking midnight."
-Naomi Klein

I write with a huge sense of urgency as our unsustainable practices are resulting in increasingly fatal consequences. We have the knowledge and the tools; what we don't have is the luxury of time. People are suffering right now, therefore right now is the perfect time to act. While we may have previously made mistakes, the next chapters of our lives have not yet been written. And we can decide which role we'll play.

"There needs to be a shift in consciousness; there needs to be an absolute wake-up call before society can actually make the kind of incredibly significant changes that need to happen."
-Annie Lennox

Many people believe that the revolution will come in the wake of a huge crisis. Others believe that a crisis is happening right now. Approximately half of the Earth's original forest cover has already gone, and every year we destroy 32 million acres more[389]. Every year we render 140,000 species extinct[390]. With our current rate of soil degradation we have 60 years left of arable farming[391], and our current fishing practices will no longer be possible in just 30 years[392]. Despair without action is not an option if we genuinely care about our children and their children. What we do right now and over the next couple of years is vital. Even if we decrease our rate of consumption but still continue on the same path, in the same system, we will reach a point where we have more people than food. We will have expanded like a virus, covering potential productive farmland in concrete, using valuable resources for short-term private gains. We would have ignored all of the warning signs and the people trying to help us.

"Growth for the sake of growth is the ideology of the cancer cell."
-Edward Abbey


Let's not allow the following Cree proverb to bear truth, "Only when the last tree has died, the last river been poisoned, and the last fish been caught, we will realise that we cannot eat money." The longer we wait, the longer we irresponsibly ignore the facts, and the harder it will be for ourselves and potential generations to come.


"Every morning you have 2 choices, continue to sleep with your dreams or wake up and chase them."
-Carmelo Anthony


Martin Shkreli, former hedge fund manager, is now making a name for himself in the world of pharmaceuticals. As revealed in a recent Forbes article, Mr Shkreli "raised the price on a drug to treat infections in AIDS patients by 5000%."[393] While it could be easy to use him as a scapegoat and personally attack him, let's remind ourselves that he is a symptom of our current system, of which there are many more.

Our current system will continue to create those like him unless we change track. If we want to solve this issue authentically we have to acknowledge the root causes. We live in a world where the ingredients for life can become privatised commodities. We live in a system where doing the right thing might not make 'business sense'. We are allowing artificial barriers to prevent saving lives. We have allowed profit to override not only ideal morals, but the very basic principles of common decency. However, we can create a world where ethics are never too expensive.


"The world will not be destroyed by those who do evil, but by those who watch them without doing anything."
-Albert Einstein

We have been slowly moving in the wrong direction for some time. We are now past the era of speculation and blame; we need to create the era of positive direct action. True wisdom is not acquired by capturing knowledge; it is earned by acting upon knowledge. True bravery is not the absence of fear, it is doing what you feel is the right thing to do, in spite of fear.

"The graveyard is the richest place on earth, because it is here that you will find all the hopes and dreams that were never fulfilled, the books that were never written, the songs that were never sung, the inventions that were never shared, the cures that were never discovered, all because someone was too afraid to take that first step."
-Les Brown

Please remain cautious as it is far easier to justify current choices than move out of our comfort zones and embrace change. You can choose what impact you have. Starting now. In this very moment. You could contribute to the problem, resist current findings, or be part of solutions; actively help, inspire others and share your findings. Please do not feel bad about spreading awareness. You would feel immense pride about stopping an injustice in the high street and should also feel pride about enabling others to stop injustices through their own actions. We can destroy the myth of the right to consume and protect more vital human rights. We can speak for those who have no voice. We can inspire others and create a world that we are proud of.

"Each time man stands up for an ideal, or acts to improve the lot of others, or strikes out against injustice, he sends forth a tiny ripple of hope ... Those ripples build a current that can sweep down the mightiest walls of oppression and resistance."
-Robert F. Kennedy

We don't have to drag the past with us, we can decide to declare a new way. We can speculate, wait and hope, or we can become uncompromisingly dedicated to helping others and creating a fairer and healthier system for our children. Compassion without action is merely observation. It is time to stand up locally, nationally and internationally. It is time to demand a new way, one that cares for people and the planet. What if we decided, right now, to show up every day and redefine what's possible?

"So many of our dreams at first seem impossible, then they seem improbable, and then, when we summon the will, they soon become inevitable."
-Christopher Reeves

Please remember we are not alone in trying to do our part. More people are becoming aware of the consequences of our current system and lifestyles. And many pioneering organisations and individuals are exploring new ways to become engaged.

"You cannot hope to build a better world without improving the individuals. To that end each of us must work for his or her own improvement, and at the same time share a general responsibility for all humanity."
-Marie Curie

What we do on a personal level is vital, and yet it is not always clear what to do or why. I know I often struggle doing my small part. I hope this book has been able to provide you with some helpful perspectives, and a potential scale of ideas should you wish to explore more options. I appreciate that it can be overwhelming at times, but I have personally found great clarity, excitement and purpose through exploring practical ways to become engaged.

"I love quotes but, in the end, knowledge has to be converted to action or it's worthless."
-Tony Robbins

We are all in this together. Your help matters.
Thank you.

· Step 1: Acknowledgement ☐

· Step 2: Spread The Message ☐

· Step 3: Question ☐

· Step 4: Vote Without Money ☐

· Step 5: Become a Game Changer ☐

· Step 6: Explore New Systems ☐

# Support

This book is part of a volunteer, grassroots movement. Anything that you can do to help get the message out there will be highly appreciated.

Every little helps.
Thank you.

Find out more at ILLUMINATEPRESS.com

# On The Shoulders of Giants

This book was inspired by a number of pioneers, and I will, to the best of my limited ability, try to continue with their great work. One of these pioneers is engineer and futurist Jacque Fresco, a leader in sustainable living and new economies. While I was writing this book, Jacque sadly passed away. I'd like to honour his great contributions by leaving you with some of his words of wisdom:

"I asked myself, 'How are you going to change all these people, they have different values, different customs, different languages, different interpretations?' So that's the time I joined the Ku Klux Klan in Miami. The reason I joined is to see if I could change them. I dissolved that organization in a month-and-a-half. Then I joined the White Citizen Council. The WCC hates foreigners–all foreigners. So I joined that organization; I dissolved it in one month."

"If you think we can't change the world, it just means you're not one of those who will."
-Jacque Fresco
1916-2017

# Sources

1. *Permaculture: A Beginners Guide* by Graham Burnett (*Spiralseed*, 2008)
2. *Beyond Self-Report: Tools to Compare Estimated and Real-World Smartphone Use* by Sally Andrews, et al. (*Nottingham Trent University*, 2015)
3. Lydia Saad for *Gallup* (July 13th, 2015)
4. Jason Gilbert for *The Huffington Post* (August 16th, 2012)
5. Elizabeth Diltz for *Global News* (January 7th, 2018)
6. Rob Price for *Business Insider UK* (November 19th, 2017)
7. Rob Price for *Business Insider UK* (November 19th, 2017)
8. Rob Price for *Business Insider UK* (November 19th, 2017)
9. Jean M. Twenge for *The Atlantic* (September, 2017)
10. *Interview with Gordon Pennycook, et al by the University of Waterloo* (March 5th, 2015)
11. Katherine Rushington for *The Daily Mail* (April 7th, 2015)
12. *Brain Drain* by Adrian F. Ward, et al (*University of Chicago*, 2017)
13. isafe.org/outreach/media/media_cyber_bullying (September 1st, 2017)
14. Jean M. Twenge for *The Atlantic* (September 1st, 2017)
15. Jean M. Twenge for *The Atlantic* (September 1st, 2017)
16. Nick Bilton for *The New York Times* (September 10th, 2014)
17. *Edward Snowden, Spies and the Law* directed by Peter Taylor (*BBC One Panorama*, 2015)
18. *State of Surveillance with Edward Snowden* directed by Shane Smith (*HBO*, 2016)
19. Rene Lynch for *LA Times* (February 18th, 2014)
20. *World Population Data Sheet* by the *Population Reference Bureau* (2016)
21. *Planetary Rent: As an Instrument for Solving Global Problems* by Aleksandr Bezgodov (2017)
22. *General Biology 2: Organisms and Ecology* by Dennis Holley (2017)
23. Nicole D'Alessandro for *Ecowatch* (April 7th, 2014)
24. Emma Howard for *The Guardian* (August 12th, 2015)
25. Kathryn Dill for *Forbes* (April 15th, 2014)
26. Ashley Lutz for *The Business Insider* (June 14th, 2012)
27. Lee Drutman for *The Atlantic* (April 20th, 2015)
28. Annie Kelly for *The Guardian* (June 1st, 2016)
29. Jill Treanor for *The Guardian* (October 13th, 2015)
30. oxfam.org/en/pressroom/pressreleases/2017-01-16/just-8-men-own-same-wealth-half-world (September 4th, 2017)
31. Erin Anderssen for *The Globe and Mail* (May 27th, 2015)
32. *Coronary atherosclerosis in indigenous South American Tsimané* by Prof Hillard Kaplan, et al. (March 17th, 2017)
33. Traci Watson for *National Geographic* (October 15th, 2015)
34. Hannah Devlin for *The Guardian* (May 14th, 2015)
35. Rob Coleman for *Environmental Working Group* (February 25th, 2016)
36. nutrition.org/sustaining-partners (August 25th, 2017)
37. cancer.org/our-partners.html (August 25th, 2017)
38. diabetes.org/about-us/corporate-support/national-strategic-partners.html (August 25th, 2017)
39. huffingtonpost.com/martha-rosenberg/health-news_b_4398304.html (August 25th, 2017)
40. opensecrets.org/lobby/top.php?showYear=2017&indexType=c (open secrets.org, August 7th, 2017)
41. *General Biology 2: Organisms and Ecology* by Dennis Holley (2017)
42. scientificamerican.com/article/stop-burning-rain-forests-for-palm-oil (September 4th, 2017)
43. Jim Yardley for *The New York Times* (July 14th, 2013)
44. Todd C. Frankel for *The Washington Post* (September 30th, 2016)
45. slaveryfootprint.org (September 5th, 2017)

# Sources

[46]. futureagenda.org/insight/digital-money (September 6th, 2017)

[47]. *The New America* by Mark Little (*GemmaMedia*, 2010)

[48]. Live on *The Today Show* (October 26th, 2015)

[49]. *The Self-Made Myth* by Brian Miller, et al. (*Berrett-Koehler*, 2012)

[50]. Ben Dyson for *The Guardian* (November 15th, 2011)

[51]. Szu Ping Chan for The Telegraph (April 4th, 2017)

[52]. Zoltan Ban for *Seeking Alpha* (April 11th, 2017)

[53]. Tim Worstall for *Forbes* (October 14th, 2015)

[54]. *The Money Myth* by Jem Bendell (*TEDxTransmedia*, 2011)

[55]. *Where does money come from?* by Ole Bjerg (*TEDxCopenhagen*, 2016)

[56]. Samuel Weigley for *USA Today* (March 10th, 2013)

[57]. Nicola Harley for *The Atlantic* (November 5th, 2017)

[58]. *The Plot to Scapegoat Russia* by Dan Kovalik (*Skyhorse Publishing*, 2017)

[59]. Faisal Islam for *The Guardian* (February 16th, 2003)

[60]. Alex Newman for *The New American* (November 11th, 2011)

[61]. 1 Timothy 6:10

[62]. *Sapiens: A brief history of humankind* by Yuval Noah Harari (*Penguin*, 2014)

[63]. *Sapiens: A brief history of humankind* by Yuval Noah Harari (*Penguin*, 2014)

[64]. founders.archives.gov/documents/Jefferson/03-10-02-0053 (October 23rd, 2017)

[65]. Stephen Goldsmith interview for *Human*, directed by Yann Arthus-Bertrand (2015)

[66]. *Our Ancestors: A Journey through the generations* by Rowena Strittmatter (*Tredition*, 2016)

[67]. esa-servicedapartments.co.uk/blog/the-new-forest (October 1st, 2017)

[68]. *A species with amnesia: quest for the lost civilisation* by Graham Hancock (*Megalithomania*, 2009)

[69]. Tamara Cohen for *The Daily Mail* (November 10th, 2010)

[70]. Lianna Brinded for *Business Insider* (August 10th, 2016)

[71]. *Who Owns Britain: Top UK Landowners* by *Country Life* (November 11th, 2010)

[72]. centennialbulb.org/facts.htm (October 1st, 2017)

[73]. Adam Hadhazy for *BBC Future* (June 12th, 2016)

[74]. Adam Hadhazy for *BBC Future* (June 12th, 2016)

[75]. J. B. MacKinnon for *The New Yorker* (July 14th, 2016)

[76]. Sendhil Mullainathan for *The New York Times* (July 26th, 2014)

[77]. Syed Faraz Ahmed for *The Atlantic* (September 29th, 2016)

[78]. Nicole Bogart for *Global News* (September 7th, 2016)

[79]. *The Autobiography of Benjamin Franklin* by Benjamin Franklin (*Yale University Press*, 1964)

[80]. Dan Mitchell for *Fortune* (June 26th, 2014)

[81]. cbsnews.com/news/ap-monsanto-strong-arms-seed-industry (September 6th, 2017)

[82]. Tom Levitt for *The Ecologist* (October 7th, 2010)

[83]. monsanto.com/company/media/statements/saving-seeds (August 30th, 2017)

[84]. Megan Griffith-Greene for *CBC News* (November 8th, 2013)

[85]. Ashley Rodriguez for *Quartz Media* (October 16th, 2015)

[86]. Ashley Rodriguez for *Quartz Media* (October 16th, 2015)

[87]. Arthur Neslen for *The Guardian* (August 10th, 2017)

[88]. J.William Carpenter for *Investopiedia* (December 24th, 2015)

[89]. Aimee Picchi for *Money Watch, CBC News* (June 17th, 2015)

[90]. Grant Stern for *Occupy Democrats* (April 11th, 2016)

[91]. Tim Worstall for *Forbes* (December 14[th,], 2011)

# Sources

92. Ashley Lutz and Samantha Lee reporting for *Business Insider* (June 23rd, 2015)

93. William O'Connor and Nina Strochlic for *The Daily Beast* (September 20th, 2013)

94. opensecrets.org/lobby/clientsum.php?id=D000000103 (October 20th, 2017)

95. *10 Enron players: Where they landed after the fall* by The New York Times (January 29th, 2006)

96. *Enron: The smartest guys in the room* Directed by Alex Gibney (*HDNet Films*, 2005)

97. Anahad O'Connor for *The New York Times* (September 12th, 2016)

98. Anahad O'Connor for *The New York Times* (August 9th, 2015)

99. Amanda Cochran for *CBS News* (March 4th, 2014)

100. *General Biology 2: Organisms and Ecology* by Dennis Holley (2017)

101. Dr. Robert Hare interview for *The Corporation,* directed by Mark Achbar and Jennifer Abbott (2003)

102. *Revealed: inside the secretive tory election call centre* by Ciaran Jenkins, *Channel 4* (June 22nd, 2007)

103. *Revealed: inside the secretive tory election call centre* by Ciaran Jenkins, *Channel 4* (June 22nd, 2007)

104. Joshua Taylor and Nicola Bartlett for *The Mirror* (June 3rd, 2017)

105. Des Freedman for *Counterfire* (June 8th, 2017)

106. *The Puzzle of Motivation* by Dan Pink (*TEDGlobal*, 2009)

107. Dr Bernd Irlenbusch (2016)

108. Dan Ariely, et al (2005)

109. Joe Robinson for *The Huffington Post* (November 11th, 2010)

110. *Does money make you mean?* by Paul Piff (*TEDxMarin*, 2013)

111. *Does money make you mean?* by Paul Piff (*TEDxMarin*, 2013)

112. Elon Musk at the *NGA Conference* (July 15th, 2017)

113. *Discourse on the origin of inequality* by Jean-Jacques Rousseau (*Hackett*, 1992)

114. *Communist Manifesto* by Karl Marx and Friedrich Engels (1848)

115. *Food Advertising to Children* by Anna Lena Hallmann (*Anchor Academic Publishing*, 2014)

116. *Anti-Bias Education in the Early Childhood Classroom* by Katie Kissinger (*Routledge*, 2017)

117. Lucy Hughes interview for *The Corporation,* directed by Mark Achbar and Jennifer Abbott (2003)

118. *Avergames: It's not an advert—it says play* by Professor Agnes Nairn and Dr Haiming Hang (2012)

119. *Avergames: It's not an advert—it says play* by Professor Agnes Nairn and Dr Haiming Hang (2012)

120. huffingtonpost.ca/entry/att-911-tweet_n_3907977 (September 9th, 2017)

121. Kait Richmond for *CNN* (September 9th, 2016)

122. Alana Horowitz for *The Huffington Post* (September 11th, 2014)

123. Hayley Peterson for *Business Insider* (January 13th, 2015)

124. Kait Richmond for *CNN* (September 9th, 2016)

125. library.fora.tv/2010/01/23/Michael_Pollan_on_Food_Rules_An_Eaters_Manual (September 7th, 2017)

126. library.fora.tv/2010/01/23/Michael_Pollan_on_Food_Rules_An_Eaters_Manual (September 7th, 2017)

127. *Grammar of the edit* by Roy Thompson (*Focal Press*, 1993)

128. *Consumer Culture, Identity and Well-Being* by Helga Dittmar (*Psychology Press*, 2008)

129. *Simulacra and Simulations* by Jean Baudrillard (*University of Michigan Press*, 1994)

130. *Brain Rules* by Dr John Medina (*Pear Press*, 2009)

131. *Neuroscience, the Natural Environment, and Building Design* by Nikos Salingaros, et al. (*University of Texas*, 2006)

132. *Consumer Culture, Identity and Well-Being* by Helga Dittmar (*Psychology Press*, 2008)

133. *Consumer Culture, Identity and Well-Being* by Helga Dittmar (*Psychology Press*, 2008)

134. plasticsurgery.org/news/press-releases/new-statistics-reflect-the-changing-face-of-plastic-surgery

# Sources

(September 7th, 2016)

135. Robin Leach for *Review Journal* (May 2nd, 2017)

136. Charlie Austin for *Top Speed* (July 26th, 2010)

137. Anna Kramer for *Oxfam America* (December 10th, 2014)

138. *Marxism and Media Studies* by Mike Wayne (*Pluto Press*, 2003)

139. Oli Smith for *The Express* (April 25th, 2016)

140. Oli Smith for *The Express* (April 25th, 2016)

141. Steven Jiang for *CNN* (November 7th, 2013)

142. Susanna Rustin for *The Guardian* (June 25th, 2014)

143. Ellen Wulfhorst for *The Independent* (November 17th, 2017)

144. German Lopez for *Vox* (August 17th, 2017)

145. Claire Cohen for *The Telegraph* (July 14th, 2017)

146. politifact.com/personalities/donald-trump (October 24th, 2017)

147. David Barstrow, et al. for *The New York Times* (October 31st, 2016)

148. hughhewitt.com/donald-trump-returns (September 12th, 2017)

149. Donald Trump, election campaign speech (June 16th, 2016)

150. Tamara Keith for *NPR* (May 23rd, 2016)

151. Tamara Keith for *NPR* (May 23rd, 2016)

152. Andrew P. Napolitano for *The Washington Times* (April 26th, 2017)

153. opensecrets.org (October 24th, 2017)

154. David A. Graham for *The Atlantic* (November 6th, 2016)

155. Aaron Bandler for *The Dailywire* (September 27th, 2016)

156. Naomi Cohen for *Telesur* (December 14th, 2015)

157. Interview with John Pilger for *RT* by Afshin Rattansi (November, 2016)

158. Sarah Wolfe for *PRI* (January 14th, 2014)

159. news.bbc.co.uk/2/shared/spl/hi/uk/06/prisons/html/nn2page1.stm (September 8th, 2017)

160. Daniel Marans for *The Huffington Post* (March 14th, 2016)

161. aljazeera.com/indepth/interactive/2017/02/10-countries-export-major-weapons-170220170539801.html (September 8th, 2017)

162. Niall McCarthy for *Forbes* (April 24th, 2017)

163. Susan Brink for *NPR* (April 20th, 2017)

164. Aamna Mohdin for *Quartz* (January 26th, 2017)

165. huffingtonpost.com/2012/01/10/first-world-countries-obesity_n_1197433.html (September 8th, 2017)

166. Mark Gongloff for *The Huffington Post* (August 15th, 2013)

167. Charlotte McDonald for *BBC News* (June 16th, 2015)

168. Tom LoBianco and Ashley Killough for *CNN Politics* (August 19th, 2016)

169. Jonathan Berr for *CNN Money Watch* (November 8th, 2016)

170. Maxwell Strachan for *The Huffington Post* (November 28th, 2016)

171. Ian Austen and Clifford Krauss for *The New York Times* (January 25th, 2017)

172. Ryan Bort for *Newsweek* (April 4th, 2016)

173. Ted Jeory and Jon Stone for *The Independent* (July 12th, 2016)

174. Paul Blumenthal for *The Huffington Post* (April 19th, 2017)

175. Andrew Clark for *The Guardian* (September 2nd, 2009)

176. Jesse Coleman for *Greenpeace* (April 21st, 2016)

177. *Everything was forever until it was no more* by Alexei Yurchak (*Princeton University Press*, 2006)

178. *Under The Skin* with Russell Brand and Adam Curtis (March 22nd, 2017)

# Sources

179. *HyperNormalisation* directed by Adam Curtis (*BBC*, 2016)

180. Dean Mathers for *The Richest* (April 3rd, 2014)

181. nytimes.com/2006/12/20/washington/20text-bush.html (November 22nd, 2017)

182. Frances Ryan for *The Guardian* (December 14th, 2017)

183. Valerie Strauss for *The Washington Post* (October 1st, 2017)

184. Tara Golshan for *Vox* (December 22nd, 2017)

185. Eduardo Porter for *The New York Times* (August 5th, 2016)

186. Kevin Dugan for *New York Post* (October 30th, 2017)

187. Alexia Fernandez Campbell for *The Atlantic* (April 14th, 2016)

188. David M. Herszenhorn for *The New York Times* (October 3rd, 2008)

189. Kimberly Amadeo for *The Balance* (August 10th, 2017)

190. Aaron Blake for *The Washington Post* (October 2nd, 2016)

191. Rebecca Harrington and Skye Gould for *The Huffington Post* (June 1st, 2017)

192. Oliver Milman for *The Guardian* (June 2nd, 2017)

193. Justin Gillis and Nadja Popovich for *The New York Times* (June 1st, 2017)

194. Tom McCarthy and Lauren Gambino for *The Guardian* (June 1st, 2017)

195. Tom McCarthy and Lauren Gambino for *The Guardian* (June 1st, 2017)

196. Interview on *Meet The Press NBC* (*NBC*, 2015)

197. Alexandra Wiltz for *The Independent* (October 2nd, 2017)

198. Jack Blanchard for *The Mirror* (November 17th, 2014)

199. Naomi Cohen for *Telesur* (December 14th, 2015)

200. Peter Holley for *The Washington Post* (November 2nd, 2016)

201. *Finesse 401* by Laurence C. Hatch (*Laurence Hatch Press*, 2015)

202. bbc.com/news/uk-41878305 (November 15th, 2017)

203. *Human Evolution* by Robin Dunbar (*Pelican Books*, 2014)

204. *Human Evolution* by Robin Dunbar (*Pelican Books*, 2014)

205. oxfam.org/en/pressroom/pressreleases/2017-01-16/just-8-men-own-same-wealth-half-world (September 4th, 2017)

206. *Monkeys reject unequal pay* by Dr Sarah Brosnan and Dr Frans de Waal (*Nature,* September 18th, 2003)

207. Kathryn Dill for *Forbes* (April 15th, 2014)

208. Rupert Neate for *The Guardian* (December 27th, 2017)

209. kailashecovillage.org (September 8th, 2017)

210. *Interview with The Steward Woodland Community* for *Alternative Living* by Nathalie Lovell (October, 2009)

211. ecovillagebook.org/ecovillages/konohana (September 8th, 2017)

212. *Young Greeks Create Self-reliant Island Society*, a report by *NTD TV* (August, 2012)

213. *Young Greeks Create Self-reliant Island Society*, a report by *NTD TV* (August, 2012)

214. *Ecological footprint of the findhorn foundation community* by Professor Stephen Tinsely and Heather George (*SDRC*, August, 2006)

215. Aaron Wherry for *CBC News* (May 10th, 2017)

216. Jeremy Berke for *The Business Insider* (March 10th, 2017)

217. *Testing Theories of American Politics: Elites, Interest Groups, and Average Citizens* by Professor Martin Gilens and Professor Benjamin I. Page (*APSA*, September, 2014)

218. Elisabeth Rosenthal and Andrew Martin for *The New York Times* (June 4th, 2008)

219. Brad Plumer for *The Washington Post* (January 7th, 2013)

220. Emmanuel Ocbazghi for *The Business Insider* (March 3rd, 2017)

221. Emmanuel Ocbazghi for *The Business Insider* (March 3rd, 2017)

# Sources

222. Edward Wong and Chris Buckley for *The New York Times* (March 4th, 2015)

223. bloomberg.com/billionaires (January 24th, 2018)

224. federal-budget.insidegov.com/l/118/2015 (September 2nd, 2017)

225. Charlotte McDonald for *BBC News* (June 16th, 2015)

226. Helen Davidson and Oliver Milman for *The Guardian* (April 22nd, 2017)

227. Interview on *The Tim Ferriss Show* (August 10th, 2016)

228. who.int/mediacentre/factsheets/fs266/en/ (August 29th, 2017)

229. climate.nasa.gov/vitalsigns/global-temperature (August 29th, 2017)

230. wired.co.uk/article/climate-change-facts (August 29th, 2017)

231. wired.co.uk/article/climate-change-facts (August 29th, 2017)

232. climatechangenews.com/2016/12/20/global-warming-linked-to-plant-animal-extinctions (August 29th, 2017)

233. wired.co.uk/article/climate-change-facts (August 29th, 2017)

234. hughhewitt.com/donald-trump-returns (September 12th, 2017)

235. *Consensus on consensus: a synthesis of consensus estimates on human-caused global warming* by John Cook, et al. (*IOP Publishing Ltd*, 2016)

236. Nicole Mortillaro for *CBC* (November 14th, 2017)

237. *Amazon Deforestation, Once Tames, Comes Roaring Back* by Claire Rigby et al (*New York Times*, February, 2017)

238. *Overgrazing* by C. Michael Hogan (*The Encyclopedia of Earth*, May, 2010)

239. *Risk Assessment Evaluation for Concentrated Animal Feeding Operations* by the *EPA* (2004)

240. *Land, irrigation water, greenhouse gas, reactive nitrogen burdens of meat, eggs and dairy production in the United States* by Gordon Eishel et al (*National Academy of Sciences*, 2014)

241. *Livestock's Long Shadow: environmental issues and options* by The United Nations (2006)

242. *Global diets link environmental sustainability and human health* by Michael Clark and David Tilman (*Nature*, Vol. 515, November 27th, 2014)

243. worldanimalfoundation.org/articles/article/8949042/186425.htm (December 5th, 2017)

244. scientificamerican.com/article/ocean-dead-zones (December 4th, 2017)

245. *Livestock's Long Shadow* by The Food and Agriculture Organization of The United Nations (2006)

246. pubs.usgs.gov/fs/2006/3028 (December 4th, 2017)

247. worldwatch.org/node/6294 (December 5th, 2017)

248. Felicity Carus for *The Guardian* (June 2nd, 2010)

249. Eric Holt Gimenez for *The Huffington Post* (May 2nd, 2012)

250. *Utopia for Realists* by Rutger Bregman (*Bloomsbury*, 2017)

251. livekindly.co/environmental-facts (November 15th, 2017)

252. *Land, irrigation water, greenhouse gas, reactive nitrogen burdens of meat, eggs and dairy production in the United States* by Gordon Eishel et al (*National Academy of Sciences*, 2014)

253. rain-tree.com/facts.htm#.WatHimC5zIQ (September 2nd, 2017)

254. regenerative.com/magazine/six-problems-monoculture-farming (October 30th, 2017)

255. Maureen Cofflard for *Phys Org* (May 18th, 2017)

256. savetheamazon.org/rainforeststats (September 2nd, 2017)

257. *The problem with fast fashion* by Paul Josephson (*Huffington Post*, 2017)

258. worldometers.info/world-population/ (September 4th, 2017)

259. worldometers.info/world-population/ (September 4th, 2017)

260. worldview.stratfor.com/weekly/population-decline-and-great-economic-reversal (September 12th, 2017)

261. James Hamblin for *The Atlantic* (August 2nd, 2017)

262. James Hamblin for *The Atlantic* (August 2nd, 2017)

# Sources

263. *General Biology 2: Organisms and Ecology* by Dennis Holley (*Dog Ear Publishing*, 2017)

264. Kip Andersen on *The Joe Rogan Experience*, Episode 750 (January 21st, 2016)

265. Nick Visser for *The Huffington Post* (October 14th, 2016)

266. globalwitness.org/en/campaigns/environmental-activists/dangerous-ground (September 2nd, 2016)

267. globalwitness.org/en/campaigns/environmental-activists/dangerous-ground (September 2nd, 2016)

268. globalwitness.org/en/campaigns/environmental-activists/dangerous-ground (September 2nd, 2016)

269. globalwitness.org/en/campaigns/environmental-activists/dangerous-ground (September 2nd, 2016)

270. Live *CNN* interview (February 23rd, 2016)

271. Susie Steiner for *The Guardian* (February 1st, 2012)

272. *Are Psychological and Ecological Well-being Compatible? The Role of Values, Mindfulness, and Lifestyle* by Kirk Warren Brown and Tim Kasser (*Social Indicators Research*, Vol 74, 2005)

273. *Owen Jones meets Rutger Bregman* (March 9th, 2017)

274. *Owen Jones meets Rutger Bregman* (March 9th, 2017)

275. Will Dahlgreen for *Yougov* (August 12th, 2015)

276. Jena McGregor for *The Washington Post* (October 10th, 2013)

277. Hardeep Matharu for *The Independent* (October 1st, 2016)

278. Maddy Savage for *The BBC* (February 8th, 2017)

279. hraf.yale.edu/ehc/summaries/hunter-gatherers (November 30th, 2017)

280. *A Theory of Human Motivation* by Abraham Maslow (1943)

281. Joe Robinson for *The Huffington Post* (November 11th, 2010)

282. ag.tennessee.edu/solar/Pages/What%20Is%20Solar%20Energy/Sun%27s%20Energy.aspx (November 29th, 2017)

283. *Before the Flood*, directed by Fisher Stevens (2016)

284. Damien Gayle for *The Guardian* (Friday 18th, 2016)

285. Lindsay Holmes for *The Huffington Post* (August 4th, 2017)

286. Angela Mulholland for *CTV News* (October 10th, 2017)

287. Susanna Schrobsdorff for *Time* (November 15th, 2016)

288. cdc.gov/diabetes/data (November 5th, 2016)

289. *Statistical Abstract of the United States: 1995.* (US Department of Commerce, 1995)

290. *Temporal trends in sperm count: a systematic review and meta-regression analysis* by Hagai Levine, et al. (*Oxford University Press*, 2017)

291. statisticstimes.com/economy/countries-by-projected-gdp.php (November 25th, 2017)

292. cdc.gov/obesity/data/adult.html (November 25th, 2017)

293. cdc.gov/chronicdisease/overview/index.htm (November 25th, 2017)

294. Sonali Kohli for *Quartz* (November 10th, 2014)

295. webmd.com/drugs/2/drug-64439/abilify-oral/details#side-effects (November 25th, 2017)

296. cdc.gov/nchs/data/databriefs/db76.htm (November 26th, 2017)

297. sciencedirect.com/science/article/pii/0891584994900302 (September 14th, 2017)

298. ncbi.nlm.nih.gov/pubmed/17993252 (September 14th, 2017)

299. cancer.org/latest-news/world-health-organization-says-processed-meat-causes-cancer.html (September 12th, 2017)

300. health.harvard.edu/blog/regular-exercise-changes-brain-improve-memory-thinking-skills-201404097110 (September 12th, 2017)

301. John Swartzberg, MD. for *The Huffington Post* (January 8th, 2017)

302. Angela K. Troyer for *Psychology Today* (June 30th, 2016)

303. Mitch Leslie for *Science* (February 15th, 2017)

304. Steven Swinford for *The Telegraph* (April 10th, 2016)

305. Ed Jones for *Open Democracy* (June 2nd, 2017)

# Sources

[306]. Bruce Lee in *Longstreet: The way of intercepting the fist* (*Paramount*, 1971)

[307]. *Effect of early and later colony housing on oral ingestion of morphine in rats* by Bruce K. Alexander, et al. (*Simon Fraser University*, 1980)

[308]. *Everything you think you know about addiction is wrong* by Johann Hari
(*TED Global London*, 2015)

[309]. Jonathan Raab for *The New York Times: Notes from the front lines* (August 23rd, 2011)

[310]. Justin Block for *The Huffington Post* (August 11th, 2016)

[311]. Emma Seppala for *Scientific American* (November 6th, 2012)

[312]. *Under The Skin* with Russell Brand and Carne Ross (October 4th, 2017)

[313]. George Monbiot for *The Guardian* (October 12th, 2016)

[314]. Richard Luscombe for *The Guardian* (November 5th, 2014)

[315]. Linda Poon for *Citylab* (August 19th, 2015)

[316]. Paula Crossfield for *The Huffington Post* (May 25th, 2011)

[317]. Paula Crossfield for *The Huffington Post* (May 25th, 2011)

[318]. civileats.com/wp-content/uploads/2011/03/20110308_UN_agroecology_report.pdf
(September 2nd, 2017)

[319]. Brad Plumer for *The Washington Post* (August 22nd, 2012)

[320]. Christopher Ingraham for *The Washingon Post* (June 5th, 2015)

[321]. Chris Ingraham for *The Independent* (June 6th, 2015)

[322]. unchronicle.un.org/article/iceland-s-sustainable-energy-story-model-world (December 20th, 2017)

[323]. *Utopia for realists* by Rutger Bregman (Bloomsbury, 2017)

[324]. Scott Keyes for *Think Progress* (May 27th, 2014)

[325]. en.fvm.dk/fileadmin/user_upload/FVM.dk/Dokumenter/Landbrug/
Indsatser/Oekologi/7348_FVM_OEkologiplanDanmark_A5_PIXI_English_Web.pdf
(December 20th, 2017)

[326]. cdn2.vox-cdn.com/assets/4571085/GMO_policy_map.png (December 20th, 2017)

[327]. en.fvm.dk/fileadmin/user_upload/FVM.dk/Dokumenter/Landbrug/
Indsatser/Oekologi/7348_FVM_OEkologiplanDanmark_A5_PIXI_English_Web.pdf
(December 20th, 2017)

[328]. Adam Taylor for *The Business Insider* (December 14th, 2011)

[329]. salve.edu/sites/default/files/filesfield/documents/incarceration_and_recidivism.pdf
(November 19th, 2017)

[330]. nij.gov/topics/corrections/recidivism/Pages/welcome.aspx (November 19th, 2017)

[331]. Christina Sterbenz for *The Business Insider* (December 11th, 2014)

[332]. *The presence of micro-plastics in commercial salts from different countries* by Ali Karami, et al
(*Science Reports*, 2016)

[333]. Damian Carrington for *The Guardian* (September 6th, 2017)

[334]. Nicole D'Alessandro for *Ecowatch* (April 7th, 2014)

[335]. Nicole D'Alessandro for *Ecowatch* (April 7th, 2014)

[336]. Nicole D'Alessandro for *Ecowatch* (April 7th, 2014)

[337]. *The Century of the Self* by Adam Curtis (*BBC*, 2002)

[338]. *The Century of the Self* by Adam Curtis (*BBC*, 2002)

[339]. *From the ground up* by Lewis Mumford (*Harvest Books*, 1956)

[340]. Haya El Nasser for *Aljazeera* (April 6th, 2015)

[341]. Robert Ferris for *CNBC* (March 8th, 2017)

[342]. Erica Gies for *The Guardian* (September 3rd, 2014)

[343]. Interview from documentary, *Water and Power: A California Heist*, directed by Michael Bonfiglio
(*National Geographic*, 2017)

[344]. Rheana Murray for *Today* (August 11th, 2016)

# Sources

345. Willow Aliento for *The Fifth Estate* (December 14th, 2016)

346. Chris Baynes for *The Independent* (July 3rd, 2017)

347. Masha Gessen for *The New Yorker* (December 1st, 2017)

348. Masha Gessen for *The New Yorker* (December 1st, 2017)

349. Hanzi Freinacht for *Metamoderna* (May 12th, 2017)

350. freeworldcharter.org/en (September 12th, 2017)

351. *Into The Open Economy* by Colin R. Turner (*Colin R. Turner*, 2016)

352. ubuntuparty.org.za/p/faqs.html (October 1st, 2017)

353. Charlotte Seager for *The Guardian* (October 13th, 2016)

354. Romi Levine for the *University of Toronto* (November 22nd, 2016)

355. Elon Musk at the *NGA Conference* (July 15th, 2017)

356. Kate Taylor for *Business Insider* (May 3rd, 2017)

357. Zi-Ann Lum for *The Huffington Post* (March 3rd, 2017)

358. Zi-Ann Lum for *The Huffington Post* (March 3rd, 2017)

359. *Utopia for Realists* by Rutger Bregman (*Bloomsbury*, 2017)

360. *Utopia for Realists* by Rutger Bregman (*Bloomsbury*, 2017)

361. mcdonalds.com/us/en-us/product/big-mac.html (May 5th, 2017)

362. Daniel Bates for *The Daily Mail* (May 5th, 2015)

363. Sophia Harris for *CBC News* (February 3rd, 2016)

364. Hayley Fitzpatrick for *The Businesses Insider* (August 8th, 2015)

365. Matt Rosenberg for *Thought Co* (March 3rd, 2013)

366. Kim Bhasin for *The Business Insider* (March 14th, 2012)

367. *Golden* report by *Public Services International, International Union of Foodworkers*, et al (May 19th, 2015)

368. Matt Rosenberg for *Thought Co* (March 3rd, 2013)

369. Graeme Wood for Richmond News (June 23rd, 2017)

370. Jillian Berman for *The Huffington Post* (December 10th, 2013)

371. *Water Resources: Agriculture and Environmental Issues* by David Pimentel, et al (*BioScience*, 2004)

372. Larry Elliot for *The Guardian* (September 2nd, 2012)

373. *Land, irrigation water, greenhouse gas, reactive nitrogen burdens of meat, eggs and dairy production in the United States* by Gordon Eishel et al (*National Academy of Sciences*, 2014)

374. ncbi.nlm.nih.gov/pubmed/8567486 (September 12th, 2017)

375. *Improved attribution of climate forcing to emissions* by Drew T Shindell, et al. (*Science*, 2009)

376. *Human virus animals - comparison of waste properties* by Ron Fleming and Mercy Ford (*University of Guelph*, 2001)

377. *Livestock's Long Shadow: environmental issues and options* by *The United Nations* (2006)

378. *Livestock's Long Shadow: environmental issues and options* by *The United Nations* (2006)

379. *What's the role of factory farming in ocean degradation?* by Brett Garling (*Mission Blue*, February 12th, 2015)

380. *Amazon Deforestation, Once Tames, Comes Roaring Back* by Claire Rigby et al (*New York Times*, February, 2017)

381. Susanna Schrobsdorff for *Time* (November 15th, 2016)

382. Angela Mulholland for *CTV News* (October 10th, 2017)

383. Larry Elliott for *The Guardian* (January 11th, 2017)

384. scientificamerican.com/article/only-60-years-of-farming-left-if-soil-degradation-continues (November 26th, 2017)

385. oxfam.org/en/pressroom/pressreleases/2017-01-16/just-8-men-own-same-wealth-half-world (September 4th, 2017)

# Sources

[386]. Annie Kelly for *The Guardian* (June 1st, 2016)

[387]. Speech by Dr Martin Luther King Jr at the Lincoln Memorial, Washington (August 28th, 1963)

[388]. Tammy Webber and Emily Swanson for *Business Insider* (April 18th, 2016)

[389]. my.rainforest-alliance.org/site/PageServer?pagename=issues_forest (November 26th, 2017)

[390]. worldanimalfoundation.org/articles/article/8949042/186425.htm (December 5th, 2017)

[391]. scientificamerican.com/article/only-60-years-of-farming-left-if-soil-degradation-continues (November 26th, 2017)

[392]. news.nationalgeographic.com/news/2006/11/061102-seafood-threat.html (November 26th, 2017)

[393]. Matthew Herper for *Forbes* (September 24th, 2015)